CHURCH, READ
—— THE ——
BOOK OF ACTS
——AND——
GET READY!

CHURCH, READ
—— THE ——
BOOK OF ACTS
—— AND ——
GET READY!

DONNIE SWAGGART

JIMMY SWAGGART MINISTRIES
P.O. Box 262550 | Baton Rouge, Louisiana 70826-2550
www.jsm.org

ISBN 978-1-941403-35-8

09-150 | COPYRIGHT © 2016 Jimmy Swaggart Ministries®

16 17 18 19 20 21 22 23 24 25 / EBM / 10 9 8 7 6 5 4 3 2 1

TABLE OF CONTENTS

CHURCH, READ
—— THE ——
BOOK OF ACTS
—— AND——
GET READY!

FOREWORD

FOREWORD

THE BOOK OF THE Acts of the Apostles might also be called the "Acts of the Holy Spirit" because it recounts the early moving of the Holy Spirit in the lives of individuals and churches. Marvelous things took place in the early church—experiences that today's churches could well profit by emulating. But some people would rather not be reminded of the events recorded in the book of Acts, especially those relating to the work of the Holy Spirit.

I once heard a radio preacher say that we should not use the book of Acts as our guide. I could only think that if we aren't going to use the book of Acts, then what's to be done with it? And what about Old Testament Scriptures like the following one that pointed toward Acts:

> For with stammering lips and another tongue will he speak to this people. To whom he said, This is the rest wherewith ye may cause the weary to rest; and this is the refreshing: yet they would not hear. But the word of the LORD was unto them precept upon precept, precept upon precept; line upon line, line upon line; here a little, and there a little; that they might go, and fall backward, and be broken, and snared, and taken (Isa. 28:11-13).

Anyone who shares that radio preacher's opinion is misinformed. The book of Acts should absolutely be our example.

Gamaliel, a great teacher and exponent of Mosaic law (and also Paul's teacher), once said, in so many words, "Gentlemen, if this is not of God it will come to naught. But if it is of God, we will be putting ourselves in the position of fighting against God, and no man has ever won doing that" (Acts 5:38-39).

Dear reader, do not set yourself against God. Rather, seek His truth. In the process of coming to understand the Word of God, do not neglect the book of Acts. It is our definitive account of the Holy Spirit and of circumstances concerning the early church.

That's why I am so pleased to introduce to you Donnie's first book, *Church, Read The Book Of Acts And Get Ready!* Each chapter—and there are 33!—focuses on the person, power, and purpose of the Holy Spirit and His relationship to the believer.

And, in my opinion, there is no other preacher today who is better suited, better called, or better anointed to produce such a book about the Holy Spirit.

Back when we were preaching all over the world, Donnie was right there with me as we watched literally thousands respond to altar calls to receive the baptism with the Holy Spirit. At that time, teaching on the Holy Spirit attracted people because they were openly seeking the baptism, so we saw people of all ethnicities, nationalities, and social statuses come, hungry for the presence and the power of God. It was a tremendous outpouring of God's Spirit and we thank the Lord for it.

Today, we have precious few preachers teaching and preaching on the Holy Spirit. That's why the book you hold in your hands is of such tremendous import. We're living in an age when Satan is doing everything within his power to compromise the gospel and devalue the Holy Spirit.

Why?

Because he knows that the Holy Spirit not only gives believers power for service and witnessing, but He also gives victory in their lives as He works within the parameters of their faith in Jesus Christ and Him crucified. He knows that the Holy Spirit's presence in a person's life is transforming and that Spirit-filled believers experience a greater love for God's Word. Satan understands that the reality of Christ Jesus is much greater as He is revealed by the Holy Spirit and that once baptized in the Holy Spirit, Christians experience a new joy, enhanced praise, peace, liberty, and true happiness.

What a joy it is for me to watch my son preach and teach, in his own unique way, on the power of the Holy Spirit, and then see the people respond and receive the baptism with the evidence of speaking in other tongues. From the number of testimonies that we receive through the SonLife Broadcasting Network, it's clear that people are once again openly seeking the Holy Spirit, and we give the Lord all of the praise and all of the glory.

It's been maybe 10 years ago, but I remember Donnie preaching on a Sunday morning, and he mentioned that while he was in the Congo in Africa, the Lord spoke these words to his heart: "When the altar which has been broken down is repaired, the rain will come." He was speaking of the great move of God under Elijah the prophet on Mount Carmel.

In this ministry, I believe that the altar has been repaired, and the rain is starting to fall—the rain of the Spirit. Just like the book of Acts.

~Evangelist Jimmy Swaggart

Jamaica | 1985

CHURCH, READ
——— THE ———
BOOK OF ACTS
———AND———
GET READY!

CHAPTER 1

CHURCH, READ THE BOOK OF ACTS AND GET READY!

"AND WHEN THE DAY of Pentecost was fully come, they were all with one accord in one place. And suddenly there came a sound from heaven as of a rushing mighty wind, and it filled all the house where they were sitting. And there appeared unto them cloven tongues like as of fire, and it sat upon each of them. And they were all filled with the Holy Spirit, and began to speak with other tongues, as the Spirit gave them utterance" (Acts 2:1-4).

The title of this chapter (and this book) did not come from me but from the Lord through a message in tongues and interpretation. It was during the Saturday morning service of our 2006 Thanksgiving Campmeeting. Just prior to Brother Larson's message, Dad was leading the congregation in worship. The presence of the Lord was so real as He moved in our midst. Then the Holy Spirit spoke through Sharon Cornell, the wife of Bob Cornell. When the interpretation of the message came forth, the Holy Spirit said three times: "Church, read the book of Acts and get ready."

You could sense the Spirit of the Lord sweep across the

congregation. As I was scheduled to minister that night from the book of Acts, I knew that I was to take the words of the Holy Spirit, "Church, read the book of Acts and get ready," as the title for my message. That night the Lord moved, with many believers baptized with the Holy Spirit.

As well, just a few days prior to campmeeting, I felt the Lord instructing me to go back and read the book of Acts over again. I believe this happened because the Lord is getting ready to do great things. So, church, read the book of Acts and get ready!

THE DAY OF PENTECOST

This day had to do with the Feast of Pentecost, one of the seven great feasts celebrated by Israel. *Pentecost* means "fiftieth," as it was celebrated 50 days after Passover. This is very important to note, for this tells us the following: Passover was a type of Calvary and Pentecost a type of the coming outpouring of the Holy Spirit. Salvation comes first for the believing sinners, and then they are to go on into the baptism with the Holy Spirit.

On the first day of Pentecost to be celebrated, God gave Moses the law on Mt. Sinai. On this day 3,000 men died, but on the day of Pentecost in the book of Acts, 3,000 were saved. The Holy Spirit brings life. Wherever the Holy Spirit is allowed to move, great things happen. The life of the Spirit ushers in new converts, heals the sick, breaks bondages, brings forth revelation, and glorifies Christ.

The Feast of Pentecost was the second greatest event in human history, with Calvary being the greatest. This event would do more to change the world for good than any other happening outside of Calvary. At this moment, the Holy Spirit came, the church was born, and the world has never been the same.

Since that day, nearly 1 billion people all around the world have been filled with the Holy Spirit. Presently, at least a quarter of the world's 2 billion Christians embrace the Pentecostal message.

PEW FORUM ON RELIGION

In a recent study conducted by the Washington, D.C. based Pew Forum on Religion, it was found that among those in the U.S. who called themselves Pentecostal, 49 percent reported that they do not speak in tongues. What an indictment. However, we must not forget the Lord has the final say in all matters. So, my response is, "Church, read the book of Acts and get ready," for Acts 2:17 says, *"And it shall come to pass in the last days, saith God, I will pour out of My Spirit upon all flesh."*

SUDDENLY THERE CAME A SOUND FROM HEAVEN

In the Greek *suddenly* means "unexpectedly." The idea is that they didn't know how the Holy Spirit would come or when He would come. This identifies one of the great workings of the Holy Spirit, and that is the sudden, unexpected outpouring of the Holy Spirit. He can move anytime He desires and anywhere He desires. As Spirit-filled believers, we should desire and appreciate these unexpected blessings. As well, this tells us that the Holy Spirit cannot be controlled by man.

Sound in the Greek means "echo," as in what happened at Pentecost was an echo of what was happening in heaven in regard to worship. As well, this tells us that as ministers, we are to be an echo of the Word of God.

"From heaven" tells us that the Holy Spirit doesn't originate from man but from the very throne room of God.

AS OF A RUSHING MIGHTY WIND

Rushing in the Greek means "to be driven" or "to rush," as in a powerful force that drives back the forces of darkness and rushes in the spiritual power of God.

Mighty means "violent." The Holy Spirit is gentle to the believer but violent to the powers of darkness.

Wind means "respiration, breeze, or breath." This was the breath of God, symbolized by Jesus breathing on the apostles after the resurrection and saying, *"Receive ye the Holy Spirit"* (Jn. 20:22). When the believer is filled with the Spirit, spiritually, it's as if the Lord Himself breathes into us.

TONGUES OF FIRE

Fire speaks of purity and refers to the help and work of the Holy Spirit in the sanctification process. This is what was spoken of in Matthew 3:11-12. Though saved, there is still a lot of work that needs to be done in our lives.

THEY WERE ALL FILLED

Notice that all were filled; none were left out. It is the Lord's will that believers be filled with the Spirit.

Filled means "to influence," "to supply," "to accomplish," "to furnish." All of these meanings speak of all the help the Holy Spirit can and does give to the body of Christ.

BEGAN TO SPEAK IN OTHER TONGUES

Tongues are a divine means of communications as prophesied by Isaiah in Chapter 28, Verses 9 through 12. It is to be a part of our worship unto the Lord. Paul would state, *"I thank my God, I speak with tongues more than you all"* (I Cor. 14:18). While one certainly can pray and worship in one's own native tongue, praying and worshipping in the tongue supplied by the Spirit presents a depth of praying, worship, and petition unknown in any other manner.

THERE IS A RIVER

I believe the best is yet to come, and I believe that which the Lord is going to do in these last days will be ushered in by the Holy Spirit. As a believer, you must desire to be filled with the Spirit by the Spirit. Consider the words of David Sapp's great song, "There is a River":

There came a sound from heaven,
As a rushing mighty wind,
It filled their hearts with singing,
And gave them peace within;
The prophet gave this promise,
'The Spirit will descend,
And from your inner being, a river with no end.

There is a river that flows from deep within,
There is a fountain that frees the soul from sin.
Come to this water, there is a vast supply,
There is a river that never shall run dry!

WHAT THE CHURCH MUST BE

"But this is that which was spoken by the prophet Joel;
And it shall come to pass in the last days, saith God, I will
pour out of My Spirit upon all flesh: and your sons and your
daughters shall prophesy, and your young men shall see vi-
sions, and your old men shall dream dreams" (Acts 2:16-17).

The book of Acts is meant to portray what the church must be. In other words, the church must be a book of Acts church. In fact, the Holy Spirit is what legitimizes the church. Without Him, there is no reason to gather, but with Him, there is every reason to expect His power and anointing to change hearts and lives.

The book of Acts is a book of doctrine carried out in the actions, ways, and means in the church and, also, through its principal players—the apostles and the rest.

Over 50 times, the title or name Holy Spirit, Spirit, or Spirit of God is used. So, the Holy Spirit is the principal player in this story. It is the Holy Spirit at work carrying out the designs of Christ, the head of the church.

TWO EMPHATIC STATEMENTS

In Verse 17, the Lord Himself gives two emphatic commands—"It shall come to pass" and "I will." We are not to read over these statements lightly. They tell us that the Lord has great things in store for His church and His people. What He started is not over; there is yet more to come. Isaiah prophesied 750 years prior to Pentecost that He would pour out His Spirit no matter what Satan tried to do. As well, He is saying, "The best is yet to come." No matter what Satan does and no matter what the apostate church does, the Lord says, "It shall come to pass" and "I will." What the Lord says is going to happen will happen because God does not lie.

To you, the reader, perhaps your faith has wearied. I say to you, "Hold on, it shall come to pass." The Lord says to you, "Don't despair, I will do mighty works and I will perform miracles for you." The Lord is not through with the church. The church was born in Pentecostal fire, and it's going out in Pentecostal fire.

IN THE LAST DAYS

The last days began on the day of Pentecost and will continue through to the end of the great tribulation. That which happened on the day of Pentecost is called the former rain, and that which began in 1901 and continues on today is called the latter rain. The latter rain will be greater than the former, for the Lord always saves the best for last. I believe the best days are yet to come. I believe the book of Acts is just part of all the great things that are in store for us.

POUR OUT

To pour out literally means to "gush out." It's like standing in front of a dam when it breaks open. It doesn't trickle out, but it gushes out. Mark my word, the dam is about ready to break, and nothing can stop it.

MY SPIRIT

The Holy Spirit comes from Christ and only Christ. Man cannot impart or anoint men. That is the providence of the Lord alone. We see preachers today over TV telling people they can impart their anointing upon others. This is false! First of all, they have no anointing, and secondly, you can't give away what doesn't belong to you.

UPON ALL FLESH

What the Lord has and what the Lord is going to do is for all people. It's not just for a select few, but it is for every nationality on earth.

I don't know about you, but I want more of the Holy Spirit, and it's going to happen. So, church, read the book of Acts and get ready!

CHURCH, READ
—— THE ——
BOOK OF ACTS
——AND——
GET READY!

CHAPTER 2

THE VISION OF ZECHARIAH

"AND THE ANGEL WHO talked with me came again, and waked me, as a man who is wakened out of his sleep, and said unto me, What seest thou? And I said, I have looked, and behold a candlestick all of gold, with a bowl upon the top of it, and His seven lamps thereon, and seven pipes to the seven lamps, which are upon the top thereof: And two olive trees by it, one upon the right side of the bowl, and the other upon the left side thereof. So I answered and spoke to the angel who talked with me, saying, What are these, my Lord? Then the angel who talked with me answered and said unto me, Know you not what these be? and I said, No, my Lord. Then He answered and spoke unto me, saying, This is the word of the Lord *unto Zerubbabel, saying, Not by might, nor by power, but by My Spirit, says the* Lord *of Hosts"* (Zech. 4:1-6).

Zechariah was one of the greatest prophets who ever lived. He, along with Haggai, was raised up by God to minister to the exiles returning from 70 years of captivity in Babylon. Their ministry was to inspire the rebuilding of the temple. As well, the Lord opened up the future to him. He spoke of both the first and second advents of the Messiah, His rejection, the great tribulation, the battle of Armageddon, and much more as it regards future events.

THE WORD OF THE LORD UNTO ZECHARIAH

Verse 1 of this great book begins in Chapter 1 with the thundering announcement, *"The word of the LORD unto Zechariah."* The great need for the church today is to receive a word from the Lord. We need men of God who have heard from heaven, and who have a word fresh from the throne room of God—men whose lips have been touched by a live coal from the altar. For too long the church has had motivational speakers, life coaches, psychologists, and the like, but today we need preachers of the gospel, men who will proclaim, "Thus saith the Lord." The church today has traded a weeping prophet for preachers who desire only to tickle the ears of people.

ZECHARIAH'S VISION AND THE HOLY SPIRIT

The Lord gave to Zechariah a vision of a candlestick, with its seven lamps and two olive trees. In this vision we will see a beautiful illustration of Christ and the Holy Spirit. As the church needs a word from the Lord, the church also must come back to depending upon the Holy Spirit, which this vision portrays.

A CANDLESTICK ALL OF GOLD

The candlestick of gold symbolizes Christ. The gold

symbolizes His deity. Though He became man, He never ceased to be very God.

There were six stems (three on each side). This portrays man and his imperfection, as six is the number of man. The six stems were connected to the center or main stem. The center stem represented Christ. When the six stems (man and his imperfection) are added to the one (Christ), thus, making seven (seven is God's number of perfection and completion), we see a beautiful picture of salvation. Man is born into sin, imperfect, and unstable, but when he is joined to Christ, that which is six (imperfect) becomes seven (perfect and complete).

CHRIST, THE HEAD OF THE CHURCH

The center stem representing Christ states to us that everything revolves around and is supported and upheld by Christ. He is the head of the church; we are joined together with Him. Everything must revolve around Christ. He is the message, He is the song, and He is the foundation.

WITH A BOWL UPON THE TOP OF IT

This bowl signified the Holy Spirit. From this bowl a constant supply of oil (a type of the Holy Spirit) was available. This is important, for it speaks of supply. Everything the Lord does in our lives and in the church is done through the Holy Spirit. Today, because of Calvary, the bowl (the Holy Spirit) is in the very life of the Christian. Without the bowl full of the oil, nothing of lasting good can be accomplished. We must have the oil (the Holy Spirit) flowing in our lives.

AND HIS SEVEN LAMPS THEREON

The heading refers to a lamp at the top of each of the seven stems, which is to provide light and illumination. The number seven is used again by specific design to speak of perfect illumination, to glorify Christ. Only with the help of the Holy Spirit can redeemed man show the world Jesus Christ. Today, the church is trying to operate in its own light and illumination. Notice what the church is illuminating today—health and wealth, come to Jesus and get rich, get a new car, get a new suit of clothes, etc., or come to church and let us minister to your felt needs, which is promotion of self. However, the bowl with the oil, bringing power or supply to the seven lamps, will only illuminate one thing, and that is Christ and Him crucified. The light shows us our worthlessness and Christ's worthiness.

The illumination that is provided by the Holy Spirit will not illuminate a denomination, politics, or social agendas, but Christ and Him crucified.

AND SEVEN PIPES TO THE SEVEN LAMPS, WHICH ARE UPON THE TOP THEREOF

The idea is that there is one supply pipe to each of the lamps. The pipes were the means by which the oil would flow. As the Holy Spirit anointed Christ and was His source of power, so, too, is the Holy Spirit our source of supply and power. There is no other pipe that can empower the church.

AND TWO OLIVE TREES BY IT

The two olive trees, one upon each side, represented Zerubbabel, the governor, and Joshua, the high priest, in their work of restoring the temple and the nation of Judah. Notice that one was on each side observing God's method of supply for spiritual energy. In effect, the Lord was saying to them, "There is only one true source of supply, and that is the Holy Spirit."

NOT BY MIGHT, NOR BY POWER, BUT BY MY SPIRIT

The work of God cannot be done by might (human might) or by power (human power), but by His Spirit, which is the Holy Spirit.

Let us learn from this that we must be empowered by the Holy Spirit and Him alone.

CHURCH, READ
—— THE ——
BOOK OF ACTS
—— AND ——
GET READY!

CHAPTER 3

THE RIVER OF THE SANCTUARY

"AFTERWARD HE BROUGHT ME *again unto the door of the house; and, behold, waters issued out from under the threshold of the house eastward: for the forefront of the house stood toward the east, and the waters came down from under from the right side of the house, at the south side of the altar. Then brought He me out of the way of the gate northward, and led me about the way without unto the utter gate by the way that looketh eastward; and, behold, there ran out waters on the right side. And when the man that had the line in his hand went forth eastward, he measured a thousand cubits, and he brought me through the waters; the waters were to the ankles. Again he measured a thousand, and brought me through the waters; the waters were to the knees. Again he measured a thousand, and brought me through; the waters were to the loins. Afterward he measured a thousand; and it was a river that I could not pass over: for the waters were risen, waters to swim in, a river that could not be passed over. And he said unto me, Son of man, hast thou seen this? Then he brought me, and caused me to return to the brink of the river. Now when I had returned, behold, at the bank of the river were very many trees on the one side and on the other. Then said He unto me, These waters issue out toward the east country, and go down into the desert, and go into the sea: which being brought forth into the sea, the waters shall be healed. And it shall come to pass, that everything that liveth, which moveth, whithersoever the rivers shall come, shall live: and there shall be a very great multitude of fish, because these waters shall come thither: for they shall be healed; and everything shall live whither the river cometh"* (Ezek. 47:1-9).

The first 12 verses of Ezekiel, Chapter 47, deal with the river sanctuary. This river is a type of the Holy Spirit. Water symbolizes the life of the Holy Spirit. The strength and power of our churches is directly related to how much of the river is allowed to flow. I want to make sure that the reader understands that there is no church without the Holy Spirit. The church was born on the day of Pentecost (Acts, Chpt. 2). The early church was a Spirit-filled church; therefore, the church today must be a Spirit-filled church in order to be a New Testament church. The earmarks of the early church were: souls saved, believers baptized with the Holy Spirit, the sick were healed, those possessed with demon spirits were set free, truth was preached, and false doctrine was exposed.

In this chapter I want to deal with three distinct points that I believe every believer must know and understand.

1. THE SOURCE OF THE RIVER

The source of the river is the sanctuary, the throne of

Jehovah. Everything that is spiritual must begin in the Father's house, the sanctuary. It doesn't begin with the ideas, formulas, or programs designed by man. That which is of God doesn't begin around a boardroom table as men try to formulate plans, but it must begin in the sanctuary.

The phrase in Verse 1, *"The door of the house,"* speaks of the sanctuary from which the waters will flow. Also, it is important to note that the door is Christ, for we know that there is no access to the Father except we first go through the Son. He is the door.

The phrase, *"And, behold, waters issued out,"* is referring to the Holy Spirit who issues forth from Christ.

The phrase, *"From under the threshold,"* speaks of the floor, denoting humility. To receive the mighty infilling of the Holy Spirit, one must humble himself before Christ. How many people have let religious pride stand in their way, stopping them from receiving all that the Lord has for them.

2. THE COURSE OF THE RIVER

Verse 1 closes with the words, *"At the south side of the altar."* These words denote the course of the river—the altar of Jehovah, or Calvary. This tells us that the Holy Spirit could not reside in the hearts and lives of believers until Jesus Christ paid the price through the shedding of innocent blood at Calvary's Cross. With the debt of sin satisfied, with the blood of the innocent Lamb of God, Jesus Christ, applied to the mercy seat, now we can become the house or temple of the Holy Spirit. Once again, let me state it emphatically: The course of the river is the Cross of Christ. As A. N. Trotter said so long ago, "Everything comes through the blood of Jesus." Salvation, the Holy Spirit, grace, sanctification, and justification come through what Christ did on the Cross.

3. THE FORCE OF THE RIVER

In Verse 7, the phrase, *"Very many trees on the one side and on the other,"* shows us the force of the river as trees in Bible symbolism signify the production of fruit in us. It is impossible for us to produce godly fruit within ourselves. Our best efforts fall woefully short, but if we yield to the force of the river, the Spirit will do what is needed in us for us to produce the fruit of the Spirit (Mat. 7:17-20).

I pray that you have experienced the mighty infilling with the Holy Spirit. If not, right now, the Lord is ready and willing to pour out His Holy Spirit on you. Raise your hands, humble yourself before Him, and in faith ask Him to fill you. Yield control of your tongue as you begin to sense the river flowing inside of you and simply begin to speak in the language that the Lord gives you.

CHURCH, READ
—— THE ——
BOOK OF ACTS
—— AND ——
GET READY!

CHAPTER 4

THE WIND AND THE FIRE

"AND WHEN THE DAY of Pentecost was fully come, they were all with one accord in one place. And suddenly there came a sound from heaven as of a rushing mighty wind, and it filled all the house where they were sitting. And there appeared unto them cloven tongues like as of fire, and it sat upon each of them. And they were all filled with the Holy Spirit, and began to speak with other tongues, as the Spirit gave them utterance" (Acts 2:1-4).

There are several symbols used in the Bible for the Holy Spirit. Their purpose is to illustrate, illuminate, and to give insight and understanding.

Those symbols are:

- Oil—represents the anointing of the Holy Spirit. When kings or priests in Israel were consecrated to their office, oil was poured over their heads.
- The dove. In Luke 3:22, we read of the Holy Spirit descending upon Jesus in the form of a dove. The dove represents the gentleness and comfort of the Holy Spirit.

- Living water—another symbol representing the life of the Spirit (Jn. 7:37-39).

There is no life outside of the Holy Spirit. The final two symbols are the only two symbols represented in the Acts, Chapter 2, account of the outpouring of the Holy Spirit. I believe that this is because the final two symbols—wind and fire—represent the two most important works of the Holy Spirit in the life of the believer. Let's take a closer look at these two.

WIND

The rushing mighty wind of Acts, Chapter 2, is symbolic of the power of the Holy Spirit. The true church of the Lord Jesus Christ is to be a church of power—power that is greater than the powers of Satan.

Without the power of the Holy Spirit, there is no reason to have church, but with the power, sinners are saved, and believers are healed and filled. We see the power of the Holy Spirit in operation during Pentecost as 3,000 were saved. In Acts, Chapter 3, the lame man is healed. This is what the power of the Holy Spirit can do.

JESUS AND THE HOLY SPIRIT

There is no doubt of the importance that Jesus placed on the Holy Spirit. In Luke, Chapter 3, we see the visible appearance of the dove descending from heaven and coming upon Christ. In Luke 4:1, the Scripture states that Jesus was *"full of the Holy Spirit,"* and in Luke 4:18, the text states, *"The Spirit of the Lord is upon Me, because He hath anointed Me."* Every miracle performed by the Lord during His earthly ministry was done as a man operating within the power of the Holy Spirit. If the Lord had to have the power of the Holy Spirit, then how much more do we have to have the power of the Holy Spirit?

THE PURPOSE OF THE POWER

The purpose of the power of the Holy Spirit within our lives is to fulfill the Great Commission as given to us by the Lord in Mark 16:15-18. To do the works of Christ is one of the greatest honors that any believer could ever have. To be able to lay hands on one who is sick in body and see him healed, to lay hands on a poor demon-possessed soul and see him set free, or to proclaim the good news of Christ's atoning work is what the power of the Holy Spirit is all about. We must have the wind of the Spirit blow again as He did on the day of Pentecost. Wherever the wind is blowing is where you will find the Lord, and that's where I want to be.

FIRE

Fire is symbolic of purity. This speaks of the sanctification process of the believer. It is our re-creation into *"the image of the heavenly"* (I Cor. 15:49) by the flame of purification. As this is the final symbol used in the text, this makes me believe that this specific work of the Holy Spirit is by far His most important task.

Though we are saved, still, there is much in each of us that is of the flesh and not of the Spirit. Actually the doctrine of sanctification is just as important to the believer as the doctrine of salvation to the sinner. The process of sanctification is a lifetime process, and it is a process that can be violent to the flesh but pleasing to the Spirit.

THE WORDS OF JOHN THE BAPTIST

In Matthew 3:11-12, John addressed this very process. He said: *"I indeed baptize you with water unto repentance: but He that cometh after me is mightier than I, whose shoes I am not worthy to bear: He shall baptize you with the Holy Spirit and with fire: Whose fan is in His hand, and He will thoroughly purge His floor, and gather His wheat into the garner; but He will burn up the chaff with unquenchable fire."*

At the time of the harvest, the grain would be taken to the threshing floor, a large round rock that sloped downward. The grain would be laid on the floor and trampled under the feet of oxen or the wheel of a wagon. The purpose of this was to separate the grain from the chaff or husk. The grain would be tossed into the air while people who stood around the edge of the threshing floor would wave large palm leaves that would create a current of wind that would blow the chaff to the edge, with the grain falling to the floor. The wheat would then be stored in the garner with the chaff then being burned by fire.

CHAFF

The chaff attached to the grain is a type of the flesh that all of us battle. The fire of the Holy Spirit is the only way that separation can come. Our works and our good intentions cannot and will not benefit our sanctification. It is strictly the work of the Holy Spirit that we must desire and yield to daily.

WHEAT

The wheat is the finished work of the Holy Spirit and the only thing accepted by the Lord. If we allow the Holy Spirit to burn off the chaff, then as grain or the finished product, the Holy Spirit can then *"present you* (us) *faultless before the presence of His glory with exceeding joy"* (Jude, Vs. 24).

I pray that your desire as a believer is to walk in holiness, a vessel of honor, purified and sanctified by the fire of the Holy Spirit.

CHURCH, READ
—— THE ——
BOOK OF ACTS
—— AND ——
GET READY!

CHAPTER 5

THE SPIRIT OF FEAR, THE SPIRIT OF POWER, THE SPIRIT OF LOVE, THE SPIRIT OF A SOUND MIND

"FOR GOD HATH NOT given us the spirit of fear; but of power, and of love, and of a sound mind" (II Tim. 1:7).

In this simple passage, the apostle Paul distinguishes between what Satan desires to do and what God can do. As someone has rightly said, "The Lord has never given anything bad to anyone, and the Devil has never given anything good to anyone." The Lord has never promised the Christian a life free from turmoil, but He has promised to lead us and walk with us through every circumstance. No matter what you are facing in your life, the Lord is with you if you belong to Him.

THE SPIRIT OF FEAR

Fear is Satan's work. It is a spirit of darkness working in our minds to convince us that the situation we are facing is hopeless. The mind is Satan's playground; he plants things in our minds that are destructive and disastrous for the Christian. Never forget that he will try to get us to believe the situation is hopeless. Actually, one could say that fear is a disposition of the mind. The mind focuses on only that which is negative, bringing us to a place of hopelessness.

FEAR AND FAITH

The opposite of fear is faith. Fear worries over what tomorrow may bring, but faith understands that whatever happens to a Christian is either caused or allowed by God. It's the Lord who directs the affairs of our lives, and who guides us each step of the way. As well, proper faith is understanding what the object of our faith must be, which is the Cross. Properly understanding the atonement then guarantees the help of the Holy Spirit, which brings us to what the Lord can do.

THE SPIRIT OF POWER

The reason I label this force "the Spirit of power" is because it comes from the Holy Spirit. Every believer must understand the following:

1. The answer to fear of any question of life is found only in the Cross (Rom. 6:3-5, 11, 14, Gal. 6:14).
2. Our faith is to be placed exclusively in the finished work of the Cross (I Cor. 1:18; 2:2).
3. Once our faith is exclusively anchored in the Cross, then the Holy Spirit begins to work in our lives (Rom. 8:1-2).

If the Holy Spirit is working in our lives, then there is a power source within us that is greater than anything Satan has. Satan brings fear, but the Lord has power over the fear and anything else Satan tries to bring against us.

THE SPIRIT OF LOVE

This presents the Holy Spirit bringing about in our lives the Spirit of love. This love is divine love or the God kind of love. The Greek word for this kind of love is *agape*. This is love that the world cannot possess. In fact, love is one of the fruits of the Spirit (Gal. 5:22). However, agape love cannot be developed in one's heart unless the believer has a proper understanding of the Cross. In fact, the fruit of the Spirit as a whole cannot be developed in our lives unless we understand that it is through the Cross that all these great benefits can come to us.

THE SPIRIT OF A SOUND MIND

This actually refers to the Spirit of self-control, which has to do with our *will*. When it comes to the will of the believer, we have one of two choices: We can will to go God's way, which is the way of the Cross, or we can will to do otherwise. If the Christian chooses to live one's life outside of the Cross regarding sanctification, then one's *will* will be overcome by Satan. So, a sound mind is a mind-set focused on Christ and His victory won for us at Calvary, which brings self-control.

So, the choice is to live a life of power, love, and a sound mind or a life of fear. As for me, I want to go the way of the Cross.

CHURCH, READ
—— THE ——
BOOK OF ACTS
—— AND ——
GET READY!

CHAPTER 6

THE SPIRIT MAKES INTERCESSION

"LIKEWISE THE SPIRIT ALSO helps our infirmities: for we know not what we should pray for as we ought: but the Spirit itself makes intercession for us with groanings which cannot be uttered. And He who searches the hearts knows what is the mind of the Spirit, because He makes intercession for the saints according to the will of God" (Rom. 8:26-27).

In this great Chapter 8 of Romans, the apostle Paul mentions the Holy Spirit 18 times. This underscores the importance of the Holy Spirit in the life of the believer. While there is a multitude of helps and benefits that flow from the Holy Spirit to the believer, I believe what Paul gives us in Verses 26 and 27 is one of the Holy Spirit's most important helps for us today.

TRIALS AND AFFLICTIONS

All believers face problems and difficulties each day. However, there are problems and then there are great trials and afflictions that Satan brings against us. They are trials and afflictions that are formed and derived in the spirit world that are beyond our wisdom and understanding. They are so great that we don't even know how to pray about the problems. This is where this great help of the Holy Spirit aids us.

LIKEWISE THE SPIRIT ALSO HELPS

In the Greek the word *helps* means "the action of a person coming to another's aid by taking hold over against that person of the load he is carrying." In other words, the Holy Spirit has been given to us in order to help us carry the burdens and afflictions that Satan engineers against us. In John 14:16, Jesus said as much when He said, *"And I will pray the Father, and He shall give you another Comforter." Comforter* in the Greek is *parakletos,* meaning "one called alongside of another to help." While the Holy Spirit doesn't necessarily remove the problem, He certainly does make the load lighter.

OUR INFIRMITIES

Infirmities mean "want of strength, or weakness." However, by the use of the word *infirmities,* many may think that Paul is specifically speaking of things physical, and it could include that. However, here Paul is primarily speaking of the weakness of prayer. The thing that Satan has brought against us is so great that we don't even know how to pray about it. We are weak in even knowing how to articulate the request or petition in prayer. We know that this is what Paul was meaning due to his next statement.

FOR WE KNOW NOT WHAT WE SHOULD PRAY FOR AS WE OUGHT

As stated, the weakness is the inability to know what to pray for. In the Greek, the definite article is used before the word *what,* so the statement really reads, *"For we know not THE WHAT we should pray as we ought."* By the use of the definite article, it is speaking of something particular. It is a specific request, yet so great we don't know how to ask or pray. The word *ought* speaks of what is necessary in the nature of the case for which we are to pray.

BUT THE SPIRIT HIMSELF MAKES INTERCESSION

Now we get down to the wonderful help of the Holy Spirit. We don't know what to do, but He does. We don't know what to pray, but He does. The word *intercession* means "to make a petition or intercede on behalf of another, or on behalf of a need." This intercession is in respect to prayer. As one prays in the Spirit, the Holy Spirit, who is God, knows exactly how the petition is to be worded and how to bring the need before the Lord. In our limitations we don't know how, but praise God, the Holy Spirit does!

WITH GROANINGS WHICH CANNOT BE UTTERED

Groanings refer to a burden of prayer, which comes straight from the heart and cannot really be put into words. It's a cry from deep within. Once again, let me say it: we don't know how or what to pray for, but the Holy Spirit does.

Being God, everything the Holy Spirit does and prays is *"according to the will of God"* (Vs. 27).

Beloved, you don't have to carry the load of satanic attack. The Holy Spirit is our helper and our intercessor.

CHURCH, READ
——THE——
BOOK OF ACTS
——AND——
GET READY!

CHAPTER 7

THE POWER OF
THE LORD WAS PRESENT

"AND IT CAME TO pass on a certain day, as He was teaching, that there were Pharisees and doctors of the law sitting by, which were come out of every town of Galilee, and Judaea, and Jerusalem: and the power of the Lord was present to heal them" (Lk. 5:17).

The last few words of this verse present a truth that must be realized once again in today's Pentecostal and charismatic churches, and that is simply that the power of the Lord must be present in our services. Only the power of the Lord can change lives, heal the hurt of a broken heart, heal the sick, and cleanse the leprous hearts of sin. The decision is very simple. We can have the power of the Lord, or we can have the seeker sensitive, purpose driven, or whatever the latest church fads may be.

THE TESTIMONY OF HIS POWER

I remember preaching a meeting at Family Worship Center in Lufkin, Texas, pastored by Jerry Mashburn. Brother

Mashburn had invited a pastor friend and his family to provide special music. On Saturday night, the brother's wife shared this testimony. She said that just a year earlier, she had weighed over 300 pounds. She had been to the doctor for some tests and had returned to get the results. She had felt a little off kilter but was not worried about anything.

The doctor came in and started the conversation this way: "I have a patient who is literally eaten up with cancer and is dying and doesn't even know it." The pastor's wife, assuming it was another patient, stated that she and her husband would pray for the person. The doctor looked at her and stated, "I know you are a Christian, I know you are a pastor's wife, and I know you are one of them (Pentecostal)." Then he said, "You are the person. You have pancreatic cancer, and it has spread to your liver and other parts of your body. If I do nothing, you have about 30 to 90 days to live. If I remove your pancreas, you might have six months to live." She had the operation and was literally sent home to die.

In a short time, her weight was down to 86 pounds, and she was bedridden. She stated, "It was resurrection Sunday and I told my husband to get me dressed, I'm going to church!" It was painful to get dressed, but he did as she asked. They brought her into the church and set her wrapped in blankets on the front row. Weak and hardly able to sit up, the service started, and the power of the Lord was present. As the singing was going on, the Lord spoke to her and said, "Stand up." Slowly, in her weakened, frail condition, she stood up. Then the Lord said to her, "Raise your hands and start praising Me."

The Lord then said, "Start walking." Then He said, "Start running," and that resurrection Sunday morning, the power of the Lord was present, and the power of the Lord healed her body and gave her life!

Beloved, that's what we must have. That's what we must cry to the Lord for. His power must be present.

What can Buddha's power do? What can Joseph Smith's power do? Show me one person whom Muhammad has ever healed, saved, or delivered. You can't, for Muhammad has no power. Allah has no power. But Jesus Christ has the power! He has the power to create this world and bring order out of chaos. He has the power to speak light into existence. He has the power to create man out of nothing. He has the power to save, heal, deliver, break bondages, and baptize believers with the Holy Spirit baptism.

We Pentecostals and charismatics must come back to the power of God.

WHAT KIND OF POWER?

In the Greek, the word *power* is *dunamis,* and it means "miracle working power." However, there are several additional meanings that are worth looking at. His power is also:

1. Abundant power—He has more than enough power to get the job done, no matter how great.
2. Ability—Jesus Christ can do anything!
3. Strength and might—nothing can stand against His power.

4. Wonderful work—this statement is actually derived from the word *dunamis,* meaning, "His power does wonderful works."

5. Violence—I John 3:8 says, *"For this purpose the Son of God was manifested, that He might destroy the works of the Devil."*

He has the power to destroy sin, sickness, poverty, and anything else that Satan can think of.

HIS POWER CAME FROM THE HOLY SPIRIT

Though Jesus Christ was God, He came as a man. As a man He operated in the power and the anointing of the Holy Spirit.

Luke 4:18-19 states, *"The Spirit of the Lord is upon Me, because He hath anointed Me to preach the gospel to the poor; He hath sent Me to heal the brokenhearted, to preach deliverance to the captives, and recovering of sight to the blind, to set at liberty them that are bruised, to preach the acceptable year of the Lord."*

Without the Holy Spirit, there is no power, but with the Holy Spirit, the power of the Lord will be present to heal.

TO HEAL

The text stated that His power was present to heal. In the Greek, *heal,* as it is used here, means "to make whole." In other words, it means to heal or to make whole in every facet of one's life—spiritual, physical, financial, domestical, and emotional.

I hope you can sense the power of God as you read this, for as I write these words, the tears are literally streaming down my face. I want His power. I want you to have His power.

I believe the Lord told me to close this chapter with the words of a great old hymn:

> *Would you be free from your burden of sin?*
> *There's power in the blood, power in the blood,*
> *Would you o'er evil a victory win?*
> *There's wonderful power in the blood.*

> *Would you be free from your passion and pride?*
> *There's power in the blood, power in the blood,*
> *Come for a cleansing to Calvary's tide,*
> *There's wonderful power in the blood.*

Friend, there is power in the blood. There is power in the Cross to handle every problem in your life.

CHURCH, READ
—— THE ——
BOOK OF ACTS
—— AND ——
GET READY!

CHAPTER 8

THE HOLY SPIRIT FELL

"WHILE PETER YET SPOKE these words, the Holy Spirit fell on all them which heard the Word" (Acts 10:44).

The story of Cornelius is a beautiful story of God's grace. However, in this chapter, I am not going to be dealing with Cornelius and his salvation, but with a spiritual truth that I feel is greatly needed today, and that is the moving of the Holy Spirit in our lives, homes, and church services.

A SPIRIT-LED SERVICE

A Spirit-instigated and Spirit-led service is the single most important thing that can happen. The whole reason we gather together is to worship, learn, and provide an atmosphere where the Holy Spirit can fall and move in the hearts of God's people. Every time we gather in church, needs of every description are represented—needs such as spiritual, physical, financial, emotional, and domestic. The reality is that the Holy Spirit is the only one who knows what to do and the only one who can bring about the miracle that is needed.

When the Holy Spirit falls, lives are changed, the sick are

healed, believers are baptized with the Holy Spirit, and people are delivered, because the Holy Spirit is God, and He alone can meet the need.

As a minister, my only desire is for the Holy Spirit to fall. I do not care whether my voice is heard or not. My desire is for the Holy Spirit to do His intended work.

PETER

In Acts, Chapter 10, Peter is the one whom the Holy Spirit used on this occasion. There is a simple truth that is important to understand here, and that is that the Lord works through people. He used Peter and, as well, the Lord desires to use you, to work in you and through you, to touch others with the reality of Christ. However, there is also another point about Peter that I want you to see.

The Peter you see in the book of Acts is different from the Peter you read of in the Gospels. In Acts, you see a man who has been changed by the Holy Spirit. In Acts 4:8, it says, *"Then Peter, filled with the Holy Spirit."* I don't believe this was an idle statement, but it was done to show that after Pentecost, Peter was a changed man. Before, he had been filled with pride and self-will, but now, he is filled with the Holy Spirit. As life changing as is salvation, so, too, is the infilling of the Holy Spirit.

YET SPOKE THESE WORDS

Words in the Greek text is *rhema* and means "something

spoken or commanded." However, one must understand that it is not just anything spoken, but only that which is the Word of God. It is a word that is directed by the Holy Spirit in regard to a particular person or situation.

The Word of the Lord is alive within itself, but it is designed to be energized by the Holy Spirit. It goes from *logos* to *rhema,* and only the Holy Spirit can do that, as only the Holy Spirit knows what is needed.

WHAT WERE THE WORDS PETER SPOKE

The words are found in Acts 10:34-43. In these verses, Peter preaches Christ as Saviour, healer, deliverer, and as one empowered by the Holy Spirit.

This tells us that the words and the message must be that which is right—that which is the Word of God—or the Holy Spirit cannot move, cannot fall, and cannot operate.

THE HOLY SPIRIT FELL

When the Spirit falls, there is life, joy, salvation, healing, and deliverance. Whatever is needed is accomplished. There is so much that the Holy Spirit desires to do in our midst. There are still depths of the river of God that the church has not yet ventured into. There is still some wind that has yet to blow, and there is still some fire left to fall.

Reader, you must desire to seek for the Spirit to fall. The Holy Spirit fell then, and the Holy Spirit desires to fall today.

CHURCH, READ
———— THE ————
BOOK OF ACTS
———— AND ————
GET READY!

CHAPTER 9

THIS IS THAT

"*AND THEY WERE ALL amazed, and were in doubt, saying one to another, What does this mean? Others mocking said, These men are full of new wine. But Peter, standing up with the Eleven, lifted up his voice, and said unto them, You men of Judaea, and all you who dwell at Jerusalem, be this known unto you, and hearken to my words: For these are not drunken, as you suppose, seeing it is but the third hour of the day. But this is that which was spoken by the prophet Joel*" (Acts 2:12-16).

As mentioned earlier, in November 2006, the Lord directed me to go back and study the book of Acts. As well, in that Saturday morning service of the 2006 Thanksgiving Campmeeting, the Lord spoke to us in tongues and interpretation. His word was simple yet powerful: "Church, read the book of Acts and get ready." Since that time, many of the messages I have preached at Family Worship Center have been from the book of Acts. As well, we have seen souls baptized with the Holy Spirit in our services. I say all of this to remind you, the reader, that a mighty move of God is coming

(Acts 2:17). It will be a move that will surpass all that has gone before. So, be expecting, be anticipating, and be ready.

OPPOSITION TO THE PENTECOSTAL MESSAGE

Recently, I came across an article by a pastor of an evangelical church who was speaking negatively of the great Pentecostal move and experience. His identity is not important as I don't know him, but his comments were shocking and, frankly, blasphemous.

In his article he stated that tongues ceased with the close of the book of Revelation, and the gifts and all of the phenomena of Acts were over. That is one thing, but he then went on to say that tongues are of the Devil, and that those who speak in tongues are, at the least, mentally unstable, and at the worst, demon possessed.

Let this be a warning to all who would voice such tripe and foolishness. To ascribe the works of Christ to Satan is blasphemy, and those who would do such could very well lose their souls. It is one thing to simply not agree or to not believe but don't make the mistake the Pharisees did, or their fate will be your fate.

WHAT THE LORD GAVE TO ME

In prayer the Lord directed me to the words of Joel as stated by Peter in Acts 2:16, *"This is that."* As I meditated and prayed, the Holy Spirit began to speak through me. It was so moving that I grabbed a pen and a piece of paper and began to write exactly what was being spoken to my heart. Here it is. Take it and meditate on it.

As the church was born on the day of Pentecost, this tells us that the true church is to be empowered by the Holy Spirit. In Acts 1:8, Jesus said that we will have power only after the Holy Spirit has come upon us.

This tells us that only Spirit-filled believers have this power. If there's no Holy Spirit, there is no power. Without the power of the Holy Spirit, the believer is of little service to the work of God. There may be a lot of religious activity but little true demonstration or manifestation of God's power.

There can be no salvation without Holy Spirit conviction. There can be no deliverance or healing without the power of the Holy Spirit. There can be no gifts of the Spirit without the Holy Spirit.

Calvary was superintended by the Holy Spirit, and Christ was resurrected by the Holy Spirit. Just as the Holy Spirit raised Christ from the dead, there must be a resurrection of Pentecostal power.

The evangelical world must come to the Holy Spirit, and the Pentecostal and charismatics must come back to the Holy Spirit. The Word of the Lord says to the charismatics who espouse the money gospel, *"Choose you this day"* (Josh. 24:15). You must choose between the silver and gold or the power of God. The choice is yours—the temporal or the eternal.

The Word of the Lord still proclaims, *"And everything shall live whither the river comes"* (Ezek. 47:9). Ezekiel 43:5 says, *"Behold, the glory of the LORD filled the house."* This is the Holy Spirit, and He desires to inhabit this temple not made with hands.

The temple of God can either be a den of thieves or a house of prayer. Without the Holy Spirit, it can be nothing but a den of thieves.

Let John's words on Patmos ring true once again. *"I was in the Spirit on the Lord's day"* (Rev. 1:10). If you are in the Spirit, you can hear a voice that says, *"I am Alpha and Omega"* (Rev. 1:11).

NO SPIRIT, NO VOICE

If you are in the Spirit, you can see what John saw:

Seven golden candlesticks, and in the midst ... One like unto the Son of Man, clothed with a garment down to the foot, and girt about the paps with a golden girdle. His head and His hairs were white like wool, as white as snow; and His eyes were as a flame of fire. And His feet like unto fine brass, as if they burned in a furnace; and His voice as the sound of many waters. And He had in His right hand seven stars: and out of His mouth went a sharp twoedged sword: and His countenance was as the sun shines in His strength. And when I saw Him, I fell at His feet as dead (Rev. 1:12-17).

NO SPIRIT, NO VOICE—NO SPIRIT, NO VISION

The Holy Spirit presents Jesus Christ, the Holy Spirit

glorifies Jesus Christ, and the Holy Spirit magnifies Jesus Christ.

This is the ingredient for power and for worship. The Holy Spirit must be present. The Holy Spirit must be desired and must be sought after.

Our song must be:

> *Welcome Holy spirit, we are in Your presence,*
> *Fill us with Your power, live inside of me.*
> *You're the living water, ever flowing fountain,*
> *Comforter and Counselor, take complete control.*

Let the reader understand that from Genesis, Chapter 1, until today, God the Holy Spirit has been moving, directing, operating, illuminating, multiplying, empowering, anointing, and convicting men and women.

To the doubters, scoffers, and mockers of the Holy Spirit and His many gifts and works, let me say to you:

- *"This is that"* which helped Moses, guided Joseph, came upon David, filled the temple, inspired holy men of old to write the Bible, and led Israel through the wilderness by the fire and the cloud.
- *"This is that"* which is likened in the Bible as oil for anointing, water for life, wind for power, fire for purity, and a dove for meekness.
- *"This is that"* which is a rest and a refreshing, helps one to pray, a sign to the unbeliever, edifies the speaker, builds faith, is a divine means of communication, and

proclaims the wonderful works of God.

- *"This is that"* which moved upon the waters, instructs men, gives wisdom, understanding, counsel, and might, and lifts up a standard against Satan.
- *"This is that"* which anointed Christ, proceeds from both the Father and the Son, teaches men, and imparts power.
- *"This is that"* which is the source of hope, gives access to God, strengthens the inner man, and gives fellowship.
- *"This is that"* which speaks through men, magnifies Jesus, illuminates truth, creates and multiplies, empowers evangelism, and convicts of sin.
- *"This is that"* which gives boldness, purifies the believer, helps in prayer and worship, and can be felt.
- *"This is that"* which was prophesied by Isaiah and Joel, is the promise of the Father, and commanded by Christ that we're to be filled.

"This is that" is God the Holy Spirit, and He is ready to baptize you with His power and might.

Church, read the book of Acts and get ready!

CHURCH, READ
— THE —
BOOK OF ACTS
— AND —
GET READY!

CHAPTER 10

HAVE YOU RECEIVED THE HOLY SPIRIT SINCE YOU BELIEVED?

"AND IT CAME TO pass, that, while Apollos was at Corinth, Paul having passed through the upper coasts came to Ephesus: and finding certain disciples, He said unto them, Have you received the Holy Spirit since you believed? And they said unto him, We have not so much as heard whether there be any Holy Spirit" (Acts 19:1-2).

The great need for the believer and for the church today is the mighty power of the Holy Spirit. As I have stated many times, everything the Lord does for us and through us is carried out by the person and agency of the Holy Spirit. Without the Holy Spirit in our services, we have nothing but dead religion, but with the Holy Spirit, the church becomes a living and a dynamic organism of anointed power that will set the captive free, heal the sick, and break bondages in lives.

In previous chapters of this book, I related to you the message in tongues and interpretation given to us on that Saturday morning of the 2006 Thanksgiving Campmeeting at Family Worship Center. That morning the Holy Spirit said, "Church, read the book of Acts and get ready."

READY FOR WHAT?

The Spirit was telling us that the greatest move of God the world has ever seen is coming. He was saying to us that Acts 2:17 is about ready to happen. He was telling us that what we read in the book of Acts concerning signs and wonders, miracles, healings, conversions, and the like is going to come to pass once again in a greater measure than ever before.

MY DESIRE

Since those words were spoken to us, my whole life has changed. I want the Holy Spirit to live and work in me as never before. I'm not satisfied with the status quo. As much as I want to see the power of God, I want to know God, I want Him, I want to walk in His holiness, and I want this temple of clay to be filled with the glory of God. I must see Jesus; I must know Jesus in a new and fresh way. My prayer and my cry is for the Lamb of God to change me, humble me, and make me sensitive to His holiness; however, none of this can happen without the office work of the Holy Spirit.

PRAYER MEETINGS

Our hunger and desire, no matter how sincere, will not produce what is needed without seeking the face of the Lord. That's why we have called Family Worship Center to come together in corporate prayer. Our prayer is not for money, power, or material blessing but for the glory of the Lord to fill the house.

> *Now when Solomon had made an end of praying, the fire came down from heaven, and consumed the burnt offering and the sacrifices; and the glory of the LORD filled the house. And the priests could not enter into the House of the LORD, because the glory of the LORD had filled the LORD's house. And when all the children of Israel saw how the fire came down, and the glory of the LORD upon the house, they bowed themselves with their faces to the ground upon the pavement, and worshipped, and praised the LORD, saying, For He is good; for His mercy endures for ever* (II Chron. 7:1-3).

I hope that you sense the urgency, set aside time, and begin to seek the Lord in earnest prayer.

PAUL'S QUESTION

In the Greek the literal wording is *"having believed, did you receive?"* By this we know that it is the plan and will of the Lord for all believers to go on and be baptized with the Holy Spirit after conversion. This statement tells us that one is not baptized with the Holy Spirit at conversion. The baptism of which Paul speaks is not an automatic part of the conversion as many teach.

The evangelical world teaches that there is no such thing

as a separate experience of being baptized with the Holy Spirit after one is saved. Now, if that is true, then the question and action of the apostle makes absolutely no sense. No, one does not receive the Spirit baptism at conversion, but this baptism is a baptism of power, distinct and separate from conversion and for which one must ask (Lk. 11:13).

As well, the emphasis in the text is the absolute necessity of the believer being baptized with the Holy Spirit.

WHY SHOULD THE BELIEVER BE FILLED WITH THE SPIRIT?

There are many reasons for the necessity of the believers being filled with the Spirit. Space will not allow me to cover all the reasons, so I am going to focus on five points:

1. Rest and refreshing. Isaiah said in Chapter 28:11-12, *"For with stammering lips and another tongue will He speak to this people. To whom He said, This is the rest wherewith you may cause the weary to rest; and this is the refreshing."* When one prays in tongues, it brings rest and refreshing to our burdened down heart.

2. Equips one for service. While faith in Christ saves one from sin, the baptism with the Holy Spirit empowers and equips one for service in the kingdom of God. We, the church, are to carry forth the work that Christ started, and as He had to have the anointing of the Holy Spirit (Lk. 4:18), so, too, must we have the anointing of the Holy Spirit.

3. Worship. There can be no true worship without the Holy Spirit flowing and working in us. John 4:24 says, *"They who worship Him must worship Him in spirit and in truth."* The Holy Spirit is the means by which the Lord directs our worship. Never forget that praise is what we do, but worship is what we are. Our whole being should be given over to the Holy Spirit so that we can live a life of worship.

4. The gifts of the Spirit. Without the Holy Spirit, the gifts of the Spirit (I Cor., Chpt. 12) will not be present, thus depriving the church of edification and exhortation. As well, without Spirit-filled believers in the church, the gifts simply cannot operate. The sign of a true New Testament church is the frequency in which the gifts operate.

5. The fruit of the Spirit. Without the baptism with the Holy Spirit, the fruit of the Spirit (Gal. 5:22) cannot be developed in our lives. The fruit of the Spirit is Christ-likeness, which only the Holy Spirit can produce.

HOW TO BE FILLED WITH THE HOLY SPIRIT

By chance, if you are reading this book, and you have not yet been filled with the Spirit, then now is your time.

Simply pray this prayer: "Father, in the name of Jesus, by faith I receive the baptism with the Holy Spirit." This prayer is a simple faith declaration. You will begin to sense words, a language that is not known to you. Now, exercise faith and begin to speak what you sense flowing through your Spirit.

Let me close this chapter with the words of one of my favorite songs:

Let Your living water flow over my soul,
Let Your Holy Spirit come and take control,
Of every situation that has troubled my mind,
All my cares and burdens onto You I roll.

Come now Holy Spirit and take control,
Hold me in Your loving arms and make me whole,
Wipe away all doubt and fear,
Please take my pride,
Draw me to Your life,
And keep me by Your precious side.

Now, have you received since you believed?

CHURCH, READ
——— THE ———
BOOK OF ACTS
———AND———
GET READY!

CHAPTER 11

THE REST AND THE REFRESHING

"TO WHOM HE SAID, This is the rest wherewith you may cause the weary to rest; and this is the refreshing: yet they would not hear" (Isa. 28:12).

The infilling of the Holy Spirit is as life changing to the believer as salvation is to the sinner. Words cannot adequately express the importance of the Holy Spirit in the life of the believer.

Everything that the Lord does in the world and in our lives is done through the person and office work of the Holy Spirit.

Every time I refer to the Holy Spirit as a person, I get emails and letters from people who take exception to that. So, let me explain that aspect of the Holy Spirit before I discuss the rest and refreshing of the Holy Spirit.

Let's first state what the Holy Spirit is not. The Holy Spirit is not a *thing* or an *it*. He is neither a material nor ethereal substance, nor is He an impersonal force. He is not a quality (of goodness, love, morality, etc.). The Holy Spirit is not an abstract idea, a universal mind, or some vague life-giving force.

The Holy Spirit is a person, a real being who thinks, acts, wills, feels, loves, and speaks. The Holy Spirit exhibits all the responses that identify one as a person. He cannot be seen by the natural eye, but His actions fulfill all the requirements of a personality.

The Holy Spirit is a person, but He is also deity, the third person of the Godhead.

CHARACTERISTICS AND ATTRIBUTES

The Holy Spirit has many different characteristics and attributes that we as believers must know and understand.

The Holy Spirit is:

- Indivisible (Eph. 4:4-6).
- United but distinct. The Godhead is one in fulfillment, yet there are certain statements that can be made for each that do not apply to all.
- Eternal (Heb. 9:14).
- Omnipresent. He is present everywhere at once (Ps. 139:7-10).
- Omniscient. He is all-knowing and all-wise.
- Omnipotent. All-powerful.

BENEFITS TO THE BELIEVER

There are many and varied benefits of the Holy Spirit available to the Spirit-filled believer. Space will not permit me to mention them all, so I will highlight just a few.

- Comforter (Jn. 14:16). This word means "one called to the side of another to help." He desires to help us in every area of our lives.
- Guide (Jn. 16:13). He will guide us down the path of truth, which is Christ and His Word.
- Teacher (Jn. 14:26). He is the great teacher of the Word of God.
- Power (Acts 1:8). Power to do that which we are not capable of doing ourselves.

OUR EMOTIONAL WELL-BEING

When Christ died on the Cross, His death not only atoned for our sin, but His death also paid the price for our peace of mind. Man's emotions at times are like a puppet on a string, with the circumstances of our lives acting as the marionette.

As a nation, we are becoming a pill-popping, psychology-dependent society. We are distressed, depressed, and despondent; however, the Lord knew how this world was going to be. He knew that at times, we would need help in regard to our emotions, which is what my text is referring to.

REST

This speaks of the tiredness of the journey of life. Satan attacks the mind, filling us with thoughts of hopelessness. The cares of life grow heavier, and we grow weary; however, when we begin to pray in the Spirit, we are brought to a place of rest. The best analogy I can give is that of an oasis in the midst of the desert. In the desert there is no water, and the sun beats down with no shade, but all of a sudden, we find an oasis with palm trees, green grass, water, and shade, and there we find rest. The Holy Spirit is our oasis. It's where we find rest from the troubles of life. This doesn't mean that the problem disappears, as the desert doesn't disappear from around the oasis. The problems are still there, but we have rest in the midst of them.

THE REFRESHING

As the rest provided by the Holy Spirit addresses itself to the present and the past journey of life, the refreshing is that aspect of the Holy Spirit that re-energizes and replenishes one for the journey ahead.

The journey of life is too great and difficult for us to endure in our own strength; therefore, we must have the rest and refreshing that comes from the Holy Spirit.

CHURCH, READ
—— THE ——
BOOK OF ACTS
—— AND ——
GET READY!

CHAPTER 12

FILL THINE HORN WITH OIL AND GO

"AND THE LORD SAID unto Samuel, How long will you mourn for Saul, seeing I have rejected him from reigning over Israel? fill your horn with oil, and go, I will send you to Jesse the Beth-lehemite: for I have provided Me a king among his sons" (I Sam. 16:1).

Samuel, the prophet of God, was dejected and discouraged. The text says he was mourning. He knew in his spirit that it was hopeless as it regarded Saul. He had disobeyed the instruction from the Lord, and his heart no longer followed God, so it was obvious to Samuel that the Lord was no longer working with him.

Though Samuel was the prophet of God and one of the greatest prophets to ever live, still, he was human. He was looking at the circumstances, and he was focused on the problem and not the Lord, who is the solution.

At the very moment that Samuel was mourning, the God of Abraham, Isaac, and Jacob was planning the greatest move of God that Israel had ever known.

Some of you reading this book are facing great problems. Because of circumstances that come over you that in the natural look impossible, you are mourning just as Samuel was. However, just as the Lord was planning great things for Israel, I believe I can say that the Lord is also planning great things for every single believer who evidences faith.

Let me say again that at this moment in time, with great economic uncertainty and great spiritual apostasy, no matter the difficulties you are facing, God is working things out for you.

Remember, if you are walking and living in faith—faith in Christ and Him crucified—then know and understand that at this very moment, God is planning great things for you. Let's state it once more: God is planning great blessings for you right now. However, we also must understand that those blessings are predicated upon our faith in Christ and what He has done for us at Calvary.

It's easy to focus on the problem just as Samuel did. It's easy to doubt and to be fearful but never forget that God has the final say in everything.

I believe that in spite of all that is wrong in the church and in the world, God is in glory right now planning the greatest move of God this world has ever seen. I believe the greatest harvest of souls is soon upon us. I believe multitudes are going to be filled with the Spirit and healed by God's power. I believe the greatest days of blessing for God's children are ahead of us. So, don't be discouraged and don't mourn, but look up for our help comes from above.

THE HORN OF OIL

When a man was to be anointed to be king in those days, the Lord would instruct the prophet to fill a ram's horn with oil. He would then pour the oil over the head, with the oil saturating his clothes, even down to the feet. This spoke of a saturation by the Holy Spirit.

THE FIVE SYMBOLS OF THE HOLY SPIRIT

There are five symbols of the Holy Spirit used in Scripture. They are given as types, suggestions, or representations of the Holy Spirit. These symbols are for the purpose of illuminating and giving new insight and understanding, but they are never to replace that which they symbolize.

These symbols are:

1. The dove (Lk 3:22): The dove symbolizes the gentleness and meekness of the Holy Spirit. As believers, we are to walk softly and quietly before the God of the Holy Spirit.
2. Living Water (Jn. 7:37-39): This symbolizes life. The crops have no produce without the water and its life-giving properties, and neither can man survive without water. Just as our bodies need water, our spirits need the Holy Spirit. Everything the river (the Holy Spirit) touches, life springs forth.
3. Wind (Acts 2:2): Wind symbolizes the power of the Holy Spirit—power greater than the power of Satan.

While this power is violent when it comes to Satan and his works, the same wind is gentle to the believer.

4. Fire (Mat. 3:11): Fire speaks of purity. The fire of the Spirit refines the heart and life of the believer, forming us into the image of Christ.

5. Oil (Ex. 29:7, 29-30; Lev., Chpt. 8; Ps. 133:2): Oil speaks of the anointing of the Holy Spirit. The emphasis on oil is intended to teach us that the Holy Spirit is totally involved in the spiritual life of the believer. Oil beautifully represents the Holy Spirit because it penetrates, permeates, saturates, soothes, moistens, protects, and lubricates. Oil also purges and cleanses and if burned, its energy radiates light and warmth.

THE ANOINTING

The great need in the church today is the anointing. The reason that the church is full of man-made church growth schemes and programs that attempt to sanctify believers through works is because, by and large, the church has lost the anointing of the Holy Spirit. When the Holy Spirit is rejected or no longer desired, then the only thing you have left is man and his schemes, which are almost always aided by demon spirits that come to deceive and then ensnare believers.

The anointing of the Holy Spirit is the only power that can break the yoke of bondage of sin, sickness, poverty, and religious tradition.

The cry of the preacher must be for the anointing of the Holy Spirit. The cry of the church must be for the Holy Spirit to fill the tabernacle with the glory of God.

As David had to be anointed, we also need to be anointed.

FILL

The word *fill* means "to be full of" and "to furnish." The believer can be full of religion and tradition, or he can be full of the Holy Spirit. We are to be full of the Holy Spirit in order for the Holy Spirit to furnish what we need for the task at hand. When power is needed, the Holy Spirit furnishes it. When help is needed, when grace is needed, when instruction is needed, or when whatever is needed, the Holy Spirit furnishes it.

Horn in the Hebrew means "a flask," "a container," "a receptacle," and it is figurative of power. Today, spiritually speaking, we are the horn, the receptacle of power and anointing of the Holy Spirit.

GO

The church has a mission and that is to *go*. Go and proclaim the gospel of Jesus Christ, go and heal the sick, and go and pray for believers to be filled with the Spirit. The true church is never idle, but it is always pressing forward, pushing back Satan's kingdom of darkness.

My prayer is for you to truly know what the Holy Spirit can do and wants to do in your life. If you have not yet received the infilling of the Holy Spirit, I pray that you will earnestly begin seeking the Lord for your Spirit baptism.

CHURCH, READ
—— THE ——
BOOK OF ACTS
—— AND ——
GET READY!

CHAPTER 13

FOLLOW THE MAN BEARING THE PITCHER OF WATER

"AND THE FIRST DAY of unleavened bread, when they killed the passover (the lamb was killed), *His disciples said unto Him, Where will You that we go and prepare that You may eat the passover?* (A place had to be prepared.) *And He sent forth two of His disciples* (refers to Peter and John [Lk. 22:8]), *and said unto them, Go ye into the* city (Jerusalem), *and there shall meet you a man bearing a pitcher of* water (this was seldom done by men): *follow him* (in a spiritual sense, this man was a type of the Holy Spirit). *And wheresoever he shall go in, say ye to the goodman of the* house (believed to have been owned by John Mark, or his family, who wrote the gospel according to Mark), *The Master says, Where is the guestchamber, where I shall eat the passover with My disciples?* (Actually says, 'My guestchamber.') *And he* (the owner of the house) *will show you a large upper room furnished and prepared* (was in a state of readiness): *there make ready for us* (has to do with the preparation of the passover ingredients). *And His disciples went forth, and came into the city, and found as He had said unto them: and they*

made ready the passover (meant that Peter and John took the paschal lamb to the temple where it was there killed, with the priests officiating, with the blood poured out at the base of the brazen altar; the carcass of the lamb would have then been brought back to this house, where it would have been roasted and prepared by the disciples)" (Mk. 14:12-16) (The Expositor's Study Bible).

The baptism with the Holy Spirit with the evidence of speaking in other tongues is God's greatest gift to the church. It is through the Holy Spirit that God works in the church and in our lives. Actually, one could say that the Spirit is the executive of the Godhead, working in us and on behalf of us.

The infilling of the Holy Spirit is a separate and distinct work of grace afforded to us by and through what Christ did at Calvary.

With the Holy Spirit, the believer and the church are vibrant and dynamic. Without the Holy Spirit, the work that could be done is greatly hindered.

In this account given to us in Mark, we are given a glimpse of the person and work of the Holy Spirit.

PASSOVER

In Verse 12, the Scripture tells us that it was the time of the Passover.

As you know, the Passover typified Calvary and our salvation. This tells us that all of the great benefits of Calvary (healing, deliverance, joy, peace, etc.) can only come to us after our conversion and the infilling of the Spirit, for power and service can only come after one has been saved.

During the Passover week, there could have been up to 2 million people gathered in Jerusalem.

During Passover, approximately 250,000 lambs would be offered up in sacrifice. A quart of blood would be drained out of each lamb. The blood would fall into a golden bowl, and then the bowl would be passed down from priest to priest until it reached the brazen altar, and then the blood was poured over it. There were conduits running out from the brazen altar in which the blood would be carried to the brook Kidron, where for days it would run red with the blood.

However, in spite of all the lambs being offered up during the entirety of the dispensation of the law, and all the blood that would flow from the lambs being offered up, the sin of man could only be covered. However, when Christ, the Lamb of God, died on Calvary, one drop of His blood was enough to atone for all sin—past, present, and future.

When the Passover was observed, the entire lamb was to be eaten, except for some of the inward parts, meaning, you must accept all of Christ and not just the part of Him you desire.

They were to eat the lamb in a reclining or resting position, typifying the rest that comes to man through Christ (Mat. 11:28-30).

They were to eat the lamb with bitter herbs, meaning, they were never to forget that they were once slaves in Egypt, unable to free themselves. Today, man cannot free himself from sin except through the blood of Christ. Man cannot earn it, buy it, or inherit it. Only through the acceptance of Christ as man's Redeemer can one be free from the bitter slavery of sin.

They would eat the meal with unleavened bread, meaning, there could be no sin in the Passover.

Then they would drink a cup of wine, with the wine representing joy—the joy that comes to man when he knows that all sin has been forgiven and cleansed.

THE MAN BEARING A PITCHER OF WATER

When the disciples inquired of the Lord as to where they would eat the Passover, He told them to go into the city *"and there shall meet you a man bearing a pitcher of water."*

There are two things that are important here:

1. The water is one of the symbols of the Holy Spirit (Ex. 17:6; Ezek. 36:25-27; 47:1; Jn. 3:5; 4:14; 7:38-39). The Holy Spirit is the fountain of Living Water, the purest and the best. The Holy Spirit is a veritable River of Life. As natural water purifies, refreshes, and quenches thirst, so the Holy Spirit purifies, refreshes, and quenches our spiritual thirst. As natural water is an indispensable source of physical life, the Holy Spirit is an indispensable element of spiritual life. As the song says:

There's a river of life,
Flowing out from me,
Makes the lame to walk,
And the blind to see;

Opens prison doors,
And sets the captive free,
There's a river of life,
Flowing out from me.

2. Men in those days didn't carry water. This was a task reserved for women, thus, a man carrying water would stand out amongst the entire crowd crossing the streets of Jerusalem. The Holy Spirit stands out. He cannot be hidden. You can spot a person, work, or a church that is full of the River of Life; they stand out.

Immediately upon the acceptance of Christ, the Lord sends the believer to meet the man bearing a pitcher of water. It is the will of the Lord that after salvation, the believer go on and be filled with the Holy Spirit according to Acts 2:1-4.

FOLLOW HIM

The Lord instructed the disciples to follow the man.

This speaks to the fact that as believers, we are to follow the leading of the Holy Spirit. Everything we do is to be done in accordance with the guidance and leading of the Holy Spirit.

When the Lord first called His disciples, He stated, *"Follow Me,"* and now He says, *"Follow Him,"* the Holy Spirit.

UPPER ROOM

The Lord said, *"He will show you a large upper room."* This pertains to all we need for life and godliness. Everything is found in the upper room. Notice that He said, *"Large upper room."* Everything the Lord has for us is big.

FURNISHED

The room is already furnished; we don't add anything to it. The Holy Spirit knows what we need.

PREPARED

The large upper room is furnished and prepared by the Holy Spirit and not man, a church, or a denomination, but by the Holy Spirit alone.

So, follow the man bearing a pitcher of water!

CHURCH, READ
—— THE ——
BOOK OF ACTS
—— AND ——
GET READY!

CHAPTER 14

THE POWER OF PENTECOST

"NOW PETER AND JOHN went up together into the temple at the hour of prayer, being the ninth hour (3 o'clock in the afternoon). *And a certain man lame from his mother's womb was carried, whom they laid daily* (seemed to be a daily occurrence which had taken place in one way or the other since the man was a child; little did he realize that this would be the greatest day of his life) *at the gate of the temple which is called Beautiful* (according to Josephus, it was made of costly Corinthian brass; it was said to be about 62 feet wide and 31 feet high), *to ask alms of them who entered into the temple* (he was a beggar); *who seeing Peter and John about to go into the temple asked an alms. And Peter, fastening his eyes upon him with John* (indicates they were moved upon by the Holy Spirit to do this thing), *said, Look on us* (Peter wanted him to hear what he was about to say). *And he gave heed unto them, expecting to receive something of them* (expecting to receive money). *Then Peter said, Silver and gold have I none* (I wonder how this statement as given by Peter concerning silver and gold relates to the modern greed message); *but such as I have give I thee* (presently, the modern church has silver

and gold but doesn't have the power of God): *In the name
of Jesus Christ of Nazareth rise up and walk* (it is not in the
name of Muhammad, Confucius, etc.). *And he took him by
the right hand, and lifted him up* (was not presumption, but
rather faith in action): *and immediately his feet and ankle
bones received strength* (this was a miracle). *And he leaping
up stood, and walked, and entered with them into the temple,
walking, and leaping, and praising God"* (Acts 3:1-8) (The
Expositor's Study Bible).

In this account from Acts, Chapter 3, we find the miracu-
lous healing of a man born lame. His physical infirmity serves
as a picture of unsaved humanity. Born into sin, all are born
spiritual cripples, as unredeemed man cannot walk the path
of holiness and righteousness. As well, it is important to note
that this man sitting in front of the temple portrays a powerless
church. The church can only be of help to hurting humanity if
the Holy Spirit is allowed to move and operate in all of its services and activities. Peter and John standing on the outside of
the temple shows us that in too many churches, the Holy Spirit
is outside and not on the inside because He is not welcome.

This chapter is addressed to those who call themselves
Pentecostal. My comments are not directed to evangelicals or
even those who call themselves charismatic. By the use of the
term Pentecostal, I am referring to those who are a part of one
of the mainline Pentecostal denominations born after 1906
and the Azusa Street Revival. Those groups would be: the
Assemblies of God, Church of God in Christ, Church of God

(Cleveland, Tennessee), Four Square, Pentecostal Holiness, Pentecostal Church of God, etc.

The reason I'm addressing these Pentecostal denominations is because that this is my heritage. I am Pentecostal. I do not use nor do I accept the term *charismatic*. My roots and my influence are thoroughly from a Pentecostal background. Actually, I am the fourth generation Pentecostal preacher in our family. My great-grandmother was the first family member to be baptized with the Holy Spirit at a Church of God camp meeting in Louisiana shortly before World War II broke out. My grandparents, along with my father, were saved and filled with the Holy Spirit at an Assembly of God church. There are both Assembly of God and Church of God preachers in our family tree. I was baptized with the Holy Spirit at the age of 13 in an Assembly of God church in Detroit, Michigan. I also attended an Assemblies of God Bible school. My point is that my heritage and spiritual influence is thoroughly Pentecostal.

As well, I want to state that I am proud of my Pentecostal heritage. I embrace fully and thoroughly Pentecostal worship, singing, and preaching. I still believe in the moving and operation of the Holy Spirit in a service.

THE STATE OF THE MODERN PENTECOSTAL CHURCH

The Pentecostal church of the 21ST century is for the most part a shell of what it once used to be. By and large too many Pentecostal churches of today know nothing at all of real Pentecost; too many don't know what the power of God really is. I can say that because if they did, they wouldn't be resorting to the schemes, fads, programs, and foolishness being subscribed to, supported, and offered to their people. To make it worse, many of the church growth strategies being endorsed and used don't even come from Spirit-filled men.

I maintain that the power of God in a service can do more to meet the need of an individual in one second than all the sermons preached and schemes practiced.

The power and presence of the Holy Spirit transforms lives, heals the sick, and mends broken hearts. This is what we need and this is what we must have.

Almost on a weekly basis, either by mail, email, personal testimony, or phone call, I hear from people who are members of these Pentecostal denominations who, with heavy hearts, tell me, "My pastor no longer preaches on the Holy Spirit," or "We no longer pray for people to be filled with the Holy Spirit." Even worse, they sometimes say, "My pastor no longer allows any public demonstration of tongues or the gifts of the Spirit."

In 2006, the 100-year anniversary of Azusa Street, *The Pew Forum On Religion and Public Life* did a study on Pentecostal churches in 10 nations. When issued, the report on the state of Pentecostal churches in America was heartbreaking. Here are the results of its findings:

- Forty-nine percent of Pentecostals reported that they do not speak in tongues.

- Many Pentecostals no longer believe that tongues are the initial physical evidence that one has been filled with the Holy Spirit.
- Pastors are no longer addressing the subject of the Holy Spirit. It doesn't take a genius to figure out that if you want to see people baptized with the Holy Spirit, you need to preach on it and then pray for believers to be filled.

THE GREAT MIRACLE

The Bible says that there was a lame man. As stated earlier, this man portrays to us the fact that humanity born into sin is born a spiritual cripple. They cannot walk the road of holiness and righteousness. However, there is something else that the physical state of this man portrays to us, and that is this: He presents to us a picture of the Pentecostal church of today. They are spiritually crippled. They are powerless. As one leader of a major Pentecostal denomination said, "It is obvious that people are coming into our churches and leaving unchanged, unmoved, and unsaved." Why? It is because the Holy Spirit is not there. He is no longer welcomed or sought after.

HE WAS A BEGGAR

Not only was he lame, he was a beggar. This is a perfect picture of the Pentecostal church of today begging for the latest church methods, most of which are coming from the minds of men who are not Spirit-filled. Not only that, but they don't even believe in the baptism with the Holy Spirit.

PETER AND JOHN

We now get a glimpse of true Pentecost. These men portray to us what men of God are supposed to be. Preacher, when was the last time you saw someone saved, filled, healed, etc., under your ministry? The Bible says, *"These signs shall follow them who believe"* (Mk. 16:17). Those signs are demons cast out, the sick are healed, believers filled with the Holy Spirit, and the gospel preached. Without the anointing of the Holy Spirit, the preacher is nothing more than an empty suit, wasting God's time and the people's time.

LOOK ON US

This statement has to do with the power of God about to be administered. Instead of us referring the needy to practitioners of the mind sciences, we should be proclaiming to the world that we have the answer to the needs of the human heart.

SILVER AND GOLD

The beggar was looking for money, but money wasn't going to change his problem. The charismatic world and some in the Pentecostal world are majoring in things that won't set men free. Money is not our greatest need. Jesus Christ is our greatest need. The Word of Faith people must decide what they want—silver and gold or the power of the Holy Spirit.

BUT SUCH AS I HAVE

What they had was the greatest thing anyone could ever have—the power of God. Let me ask you, what do you have? Is it religion or the power of the Holy Spirit? Works or grace? Celebrate Recovery or God the Holy Spirit?

IN THE NAME OF JESUS CHRIST OF NAZARETH

The name of Jesus is our power of attorney to use against the powers of darkness and the results of the power of darkness. The name of Jesus backed by the power and anointing of the Holy Spirit changes everything.

THE RESULT

Immediately, his ankle bones received strength, and he began walking, leaping, and praising God. This is the power of Pentecost, and this—and only this—is all we need.

It's time the Pentecostal church and its leaders come back to the Holy Spirit.

CHURCH, READ
—— THE ——
BOOK OF ACTS
—— AND ——
GET READY!

CHAPTER 15

THE BENEFITS OF SPEAKING
IN OTHER TONGUES

"I THANK MY GOD, I speak with tongues more than you all" (I Cor. 14:18).

As salvation is God's greatest gift to the world, so, too, is the infilling of the Holy Spirit to the believer.

In I Corinthians, Chapter 14, the apostle Paul is giving instructions regarding the use of the eighth and ninth gifts of the Spirit (tongues and interpretation of tongues) in the local assembly. For clarification, when we say "gift of tongues," we are not addressing ourselves, and neither was Paul addressing himself, to the speaking with tongues that takes place when one is baptized with the Holy Spirit (Acts, Chpts. 2, 10, 19). Neither are we speaking of those who exercise their prayer language of speaking in tongues in prayer and worship. The gift of tongues is an utterance in tongues given in a public meeting that is meant to be interpreted.

One must understand that the gifts of the Spirit were brand-new, having only begun on the day of Pentecost. While the gifts were obvious in the Old Testament, with the exception of tongues and interpretation of tongues, still, they were not as widespread and had actually only been used by a few.

Of all the gifts, tongues was the most prominent and exotic. Consequently, more people wanted this gift, thereby, yielding to the Holy Spirit to a greater degree, causing an unbalance in the early church. As well, there was no regulation in the early church regarding how this gift should be used, which resulted in confusion. So, the apostle was simply telling them, and us, that everyone should not desire the gift of tongues, but rather that they might have the gift of prophecy (I Cor. 14:1).

There is a difference in tongues, as it regards one's own personal prayer language, and the gift of tongues. While every Spirit-filled believer speaks in tongues, not every Spirit-filled believer has the gift of tongues.

WHAT GOOD IS IT?

Today, some question the tongues experience, asking, "What good is it?" To answer that, we go to the Scriptures to find the answer, and here is what we find:

1. The Lord spoke through the prophet Isaiah nearly 800 years before the day of Pentecost and said, *"For with stammering lips and another tongue will He speak to His people"* (Isa. 28:11). Of course, anything that God said is important and is to be heeded by all of His followers.

2. The last words spoken by our Lord to His disciples were the commandments given in Acts 1:4-5, *"And,*

being assembled together with them, commanded them that they should not depart from Jerusalem, but wait for the promise of the Father, which, said He, you have heard of Me. For John truly baptized with water; but you shall be baptized with the Holy Spirit not many days hence."

So, anyone who would wonder what good it is, in effect, is saying that the Lord doesn't know what He is doing. Tongues are important and beneficial to every believer. Let's look at some of the benefits of speaking in tongues, with the understanding that in this chapter, I am not covering all of the benefits due to space, but only those that I feel stand out in importance and benefit:

- *"He who speaks in an unknown tongue edifies himself"* (I Cor. 14:4). The word *edified* or *edifieth* means to "build up," to "comfort," to "encourage," to "give strength." A good analogy is a car battery. At times a battery's power will begin to wane, and it must be recharged. So, too, in life, sometimes our own spiritual battery gets weak and needs recharging. This happens when one prays in tongues.

- *"For he who speaks in an unknown tongue speaks not unto men, but unto God"* (I Cor. 14:2). This tells us that tongues, as a prayer language, is a divine means of communication between the speaker and God.

- *"We do hear them speak in our tongues the wonderful works of God"* (Acts 2:11). When we pray in tongues, we are magnifying the works of God. It is praise unto the Lord for those great things the Lord has done and is doing.

- *"But you, beloved, building up yourselves on your most holy faith, praying in the holy spirit"* (Jude, Vs. 20). When one prays in the Spirit, the faith one has is enlarged and developed. I think it goes without saying that all of us need our faith enlarged.

- *"Wherefore tongues are for a sign, not to them who believe, but to them who believe not"* (I Cor. 14:22). This refers to the fact that praying in tongues is a sign to unbelievers that they will face the judgment of God unless they repent of their sins. The idea of this verse, concerning judgment and tongues as a sign, pertains to Isaiah's prophecy of judgment on backsliding Judah (Isa. 5:28).

- *"This is the rest wherewith you may cause the weary to rest"* (Isa. 28:12). *Weary* in the Hebrew means "languid," "faint," and "thirsty." In this journey of life, we become faint, tired, and beaten down. *Rest* in the Hebrew, as it is first used in the text, means "resting place." The second time *rest* is used in this text, it means to "settle down." This carries the idea of physical edification. We are weary and tired, but praying in the Spirit brings us to a resting place.

- *"And this is the refreshing"* (Isa. 28:12). *Refreshing* in the Hebrew means to "find ease," and "make to rest." This carries the idea of something being tossed violently, such as a ship in a storm at sea, and then settling down. It speaks of the mental turmoil that is brought on by the cares of life being settled down or calmed. Praying in the Spirit is God's mental therapy. This is the answer for the cares of life that vex and frustrate us.

- *"For if I pray in an unknown tongue, my spirit prays"* (I Cor. 14:14). One's spirit praying is the highest form of prayer and worship that a believer can engage in. It comes from a person's spirit and not one's mind.

BIBLE PROPHECY FULFILLED

I want to close this chapter with this final thought: Speaking in tongues is the fulfillment of Bible prophecy. In Acts 2:17-18, it says, *"And it shall come to pass in the last days, says God, I will pour out of My Spirit upon all flesh: and your sons and your daughters shall prophesy, and your young men shall see visions, and your old men shall dream dreams: and on My servants and on My handmaidens I will pour out in those days of My Spirit; and they shall prophesy."*

I thank God that I can say as Paul did, *"I thank my God, I speak with tongues."*

CHURCH, READ

— THE —

BOOK OF ACTS

—AND—

GET READY!

CHAPTER 16

THE SPIRIT OF THE LORD IS UPON ME

"*AND HE CAME TO Nazareth, where He had been brought up* (makes vivid the fact that Jesus was very man, even as He was very God)*: and, as His custom was* (in our language presently, He was faithful to church), *He went into the synagogue on the Sabbath day, and stood up for to read* (it was common to ask visitors to expound on the Word). *And there was delivered unto Him the book* (scroll) *of the prophet Isaiah. And when He had opened the book, He found the place where it was written* (Isa. 61:1). *The Spirit of the Lord is upon Me* (we learn here of the absolute necessity of the person and work of the Holy Spirit within our lives), *because He has anointed Me* (Jesus is the ultimate Anointed One; consequently, the anointing of the Holy Spirit actually belongs to Christ, and the anointing we have actually comes by His authority [Jn. 16:14]) *to preach the gospel to the poor* (the poor in spirit); *He has sent Me to heal the brokenhearted* (sin breaks the heart, or else is responsible for it being broken; only Jesus can heal this malady), *to preach deliverance to the captives* (if it is to be noticed, He didn't say to 'deliver the captives,' but rather 'preach deliverance,' which refers to the Cross [Jn. 8:32]), *and recovering of sigh to the blind* (the gospel opens the eyes of those who are spiritually blind), *to set at liberty them who are bruised* (the vicissitudes of life at times place a person in a mental or spiritual prison; the Lord alone, and through what He did at the Cross, can open this prison door)" (Lk. 4:16-18) (The Expositor's Study Bible).

It is impossible to separate the Holy Spirit from the life and ministry of the Lord. Though He was God during His time on earth, He was also a man. It was as man, flesh and blood, that He lived and ministered—a man full of the Holy Spirit. Every single aspect of His life was directed by the Holy Spirit from His birth to His resurrection.

Concerning His birth, in Matthew 1:18, the Bible says, *"She was found with child of the Holy Spirit."* Luke 1:35, speaking of Mary said, *"The Holy Spirit shall come upon you."*

At His baptism at the Jordan River, we see the Holy Spirit likened to a dove coming down and lighting upon Him.

At Calvary the Holy Spirit watched over and superintended every aspect, and, of course, it was the Holy Spirit who raised Him from the dead in resurrection power.

Even before I get into the subject matter of the anointing, I must state that I feel it is impossible for a believer to look at the life and ministry of Christ and not see the importance of the Holy Spirit.

Being a Pentecostal, I'm ashamed at the so-called Pentecostal churches de-emphasizing the role and help of the Holy

Spirit. Without the Holy Spirit, there is no church, no power, and no anointing. Simply put, without the Holy Spirit, all that you are left with is dead religion.

Luke, Chapter 4, gives to us one of the most concise teachings on the Holy Spirit and the life and ministry of the Lord.

FULL OF THE HOLY SPIRIT

Luke 4:1 says, *"And Jesus being full of the Holy Spirit."* The word *full* means "without measure," meaning that the Lord was full of the Holy Spirit to a degree greater than anyone else. The reason was that Christ was perfect and pure, while we are not. *Full* also means "to be in complete control." Kenneth Wuest, the noted 20th century Greek scholar, translates it this way: "And Jesus in the complete control of the Holy Spirit."

All of this tells us that it's the desire of the Holy Spirit to have complete control over us in every situation of our lives. We must never forget that something is going to control us— religion, the flesh, or God the Holy Spirit.

The control the Holy Spirit desires is not automatic. His control can only happen as we yield ourselves to Him every day. He doesn't force His will as He is not a dictator lording over us, but He is the dove, gentle and meek, desiring of us to want His help.

LED BY THE SPIRIT

The latter part of Verse 1 says, *"Was led by the Spirit into the wilderness.*" Wuest translates it this way: "Continually being led." In John 16:13, Jesus, speaking of the role of the Holy Spirit in our lives, said, *"He will guide you into all truth."* This life we live is one of many pitfalls, snares of Satan, journeys through the valley of the shadow of death, storms, and hardships. At times we don't know what to do or where to go, but the Holy Spirit does. He knows exactly what to do, and even if it is through the wilderness, He will see us safely through.

THE POWER OF THE SPIRIT

Luke 4:14 says, *"And Jesus returned in the power of the Spirit."* Power in the Greek is *dunamis,* and it means "miracle-working power." The power of the Spirit was His strength, and, likewise, it is to be our strength. The modern Pentecostal church has by and large lost the power of the Holy Spirit. Instead of the altar and the name of Jesus, we have become a giant referral system, referring the broken and bound to psychologists, counseling, and therapists. The Holy Spirit is power—power greater than sin, sickness, demons, or whatever force one may face. Without the power of the Holy Spirit, the church is nothing more than dead men's bones, but with the Holy Spirit, the church becomes a living dynamo, pulsating with power.

THE SPIRIT OF THE LORD IS UPON ME

This statement gives us a clear definition of the Trinity.

The Holy Spirit is spoken of, with the name *Lord,* referring to God the Father, and with the pronoun *Me* referring to Jesus Christ as the one anointed.

BECAUSE HE HAS ANOINTED ME

This anointing was a spiritual anointing and not a physical anointing as was common in the Old Testament. It refers to a special appointment or commission by God that sets a person apart. The word *anointed* means "to smear or rub with oil, i.e. (by implication) to consecrate to an office or religious service."

It is important to note that the anointing of the Holy Spirit belongs to Christ and not man. Man cannot impart the Holy Spirit to another; that is in the domain of the Lord.

THE LESSON FOR US

If the Lord Jesus had to be full of the Spirit, if the Lord Jesus had to be led by the Spirit, if the Lord Jesus had to have the power of the Spirit, and if the Lord Jesus had to have the anointing of the Holy Spirit, then how much more do we who are flawed and imperfect have to have the Holy Spirit?

You need the anointing to be the best husband, wife, father, mother, son, daughter, student, employer, or employee.

Every one of us needs to be able to say, *"The Spirit of the Lord is upon me because He has anointed me."*

CHURCH, READ
—— THE ——
BOOK OF ACTS
——AND——
GET READY!

CHAPTER 17

HE HAS ANOINTED ME TO
PREACH THE GOSPEL

"AND HE CAME TO Nazareth, where He had been brought up (makes vivid the fact that Jesus was very man, even as He was very God)*: and, as His custom was* (in our language presently He was faithful to church)*, He went into the synagogue on the Sabbath day, and stood up for to read* (it was common to ask visitors to expound on the Word). *And there was delivered unto Him the book* (scroll) *of the prophet Isaiah. And when He had opened the book, He found the place where it was written* (Isa. 61:1), *The Spirit of the Lord is upon Me* (we learn here of the absolute necessity of the person and work of the Holy Spirit within our lives)*, because He has anointed Me* (Jesus is the ultimate Anointed One; consequently, the anointing of the Holy Spirit actually belongs to Christ, and the anointing we have actually comes by His authority [Jn. 16:14]) *to preach the gospel to the poor* (the poor in spirit)*; He has sent Me to heal the brokenhearted* (sin breaks the heart, or else is responsible for it being broken; only Jesus can heal this malady)*, to preach deliverance to the captives* (if it is to be noticed, He

didn't say to 'deliver the captives,' but rather 'preach deliverance,' which refers to the Cross [Jn. 8:32]), *and recovering of sight to the blind* (the gospel opens the eyes of those who are spiritually blind), *to set at liberty them who are bruised* (the vicissitudes of life at times place a person in a mental or spiritual prison; the Lord alone, and through what He did at the Cross, can open this prison door)" (Lk. 4:16-18) (The Expositor's Study Bible).

In the last chapter, I dealt with the first part of Christ's statement, *"The Spirit of the Lord is upon Me."* I feel it is necessary to recap some important points:

1. You can't separate the Holy Spirit from the life and ministry of Jesus Christ. Everything the Lord did while on earth was as a man full of the Holy Spirit.

2. Luke 4:1 says, *"And Jesus being full of the Holy Spirit."* The word *full* means "without measure" and "to be in complete control." The Holy Spirit desires to be in total and absolute control of our lives.

3. He was *"led by the Spirit"* (Lk. 4:1), meaning "continually being led" by the Spirit. The Spirit desires to have control in order to continually lead us in our walk with the Lord.

4. Luke 4:14 says, *"Jesus returned in the power of the (Holy) Spirit."* Power in the Greek is *dunamis* and means "miracle-working power." This was His strength (the power of the Holy Spirit), and it must be our strength as well.

THE ANOINTING

Now we come to the subject of our text, *"He has anointed Me."* This statement speaks of a spiritual anointing. This statement also tells us that the anointing of the Holy Spirit belongs to Christ and not man.

By that I mean that man cannot give the anointing to other men; that is the domain of the Lord alone. We often see on TV a preacher telling people that he can impart whatever degree of anointing he supposedly has to others, usually for a fee. This is false, and it is sin. The anointing is not a commodity that can be sold, but it is a work of grace and the Spirit given to men by the Lord according to the hunger and consecration of the individual.

THE NEED FOR TODAY

The great need for the church today is preachers who have the anointing of the Holy Spirit upon their lives and ministries. It's sad, but too much that is presented as the gospel is nothing more than man's intellect at best and shamanism at worst.

Education and intellect will not set the captive free. Good humor and a pleasing personality will not see the sick healed. What we need are preachers who have the anointing of the Holy Spirit upon them: men and women who, when they preach, proclaim the oracles of God, and men and women who preach the truth of God's Word with conviction and without fear.

TO PREACH THE GOSPEL

The anointing is needed to carry out specific tasks. In the case of the Lord, He was anointed to preach the gospel. Preaching means "to proclaim or herald." It doesn't necessarily refer to style or animation but to content. What one has to say is more important than how one says it. Never forget that the Holy Spirit always has something to say, and it's our responsibility to hear His voice and then to deliver what He wants said. The word *gospel* means "good news," the good news of God's Word taken to the heart of souls in need of help.

As a minister of the gospel, I am a *"watchman"* (Ezek. 3:17; 33:7). I am not a diplomat, and I am not a politician, but I am a proclaimer of God's Word. It is my job to stand upon the wall of the church and to sound the alarm. I don't preach what I think will make me popular, rich, famous, etc., but I am to preach "thus saith the Lord," regardless of whether it's accepted or rejected.

The church has lost its way because of what is being preached and because the anointing has been lost. You can tell the spiritual condition of a denomination by the caliber of the preachers it produces.

WHAT TYPE OF GOSPEL WAS JESUS SPEAKING OF?

The answer to the question of the heading can be summed up by these words: Jesus saves, Jesus heals, Jesus baptizes with the Holy Spirit, and Jesus is coming soon.

All preaching should focus upon who Jesus is and what Jesus has done and will do in people's hearts. The true gospel of Jesus Christ includes salvation for the soul, healing for the body, and the overcoming power and victory by the Holy Spirit for the believer. Let us seek the Lord for His anointing in order to help humanity find its way.

CHURCH, READ
—— THE ——
BOOK OF ACTS
—— AND ——
GET READY!

CHAPTER 18

THERE IS A RIVER

"AFTERWARD HE BROUGHT ME again unto the door of the house; and, behold, waters issued out from under the threshold of the house eastward: for the forefront of the house stood toward the east, and the waters came down from under from the right side of the house, at the south side of the altar." (Ezek. 47:1).

Ezekiel was a priest and a prophet. His messages were given by the Lord to exiles in Babylonia. His prophecies were wide-ranging, covering events all the way from the fall of Jerusalem to its restoration, which is yet to come. He was given visions into the Spirit world that are equaled only by that given to John on the isle of Patmos.

Ezekiel saw the glory of God leave the temple as Israel lost her way, but he also saw the coming day when the Spirit of God would return to the temple during the millennial reign of Jesus Christ. Actually, he is often referred to as the millennial prophet due to his glorious visions of that great day to come.

Chapters 40 through 48 of Ezekiel deal with the temple of God that will be built in the coming kingdom age.

In Chapter 47, we are given a glimpse of the river of the sanctuary, which serves as a type of the Holy Spirit.

THE DOOR

The phrase of Verse 1, *"Afterward He brought me again unto the door of the house,"* speaks of the sanctuary from which these waters will flow. There are two biblical types found in this phrase. *"The house"* is the sanctuary, which serves as a type of God the Father, and *"the door"* represents Christ, telling us that the only way to the Father is through the door, His Son, Jesus Christ.

THE WATERS

The phrase, *"And, behold, waters issued out from under the threshold of the house eastward,"* proclaims a symbolism of the Holy Spirit, of which water is a type, representing the life of the Holy Spirit—living water.

This serves as a symbolic fulfillment of the words of our Lord when He said, *"If any man thirst, let him come unto Me, and drink. He who believes on Me, as the Scripture has said, out of his belly* (innermost being) *shall flow rivers of living water. (But this spoke He of the Spirit)"* (Jn. 7:37-39).

As stated, water is a symbol of the Holy Spirit for life. The Holy Spirit is the fountain of living water; He is a veritable River of Life, flooding and gushing over our souls. This water purifies, refreshes, and makes fruitful. As literal water is indispensable to us for physical life, so, too, is the river of the Spirit indispensable to our spiritual life.

Without the Holy Spirit—the River of Life—church is just a religious exercise that will profit no man, but if the river that flows from the sanctuary is welcome and is flowing, then a dead, cold, religious service becomes a living organism of power.

If the river flows, then the sinner can be saved, the sick body healed, the broken heart mended, believers can be filled with the Holy Spirit, and the Word of God can literally come alive to the human heart. Simply put, if the waters that flow from the sanctuary are not in your church, then you have no church.

The river began to flow on the day of Pentecost (Acts, Chpt. 2) and has been flowing ever since. As the church was born on the day of Pentecost, this tells us that it is God's will for the power of Pentecost to flow unhindered and uninterrupted in the church of today.

The modern Pentecostal and charismatic churches have by and large apostatized and have forsaken *"the fountain of living waters, and hewed them out cisterns, broken cisterns, that can hold no water"* (Jer. 2:13). I can say that because of what they are offering the people: psychology, works, schemes, and plans from the minds of men. You can either drink and live in the waters of the sanctuary, or you can drink from the stagnant water that flows from the hearts of men who are no longer flowing in the Holy Spirit.

According to the latest statistics, the major Pentecostal denominations (the Assemblies of God, Foursquare, etc.) can no longer truly call themselves Pentecostal, as they no longer can say that an overwhelming majority of their membership speaks in tongues. As mentioned earlier, the *Pew Forum on Religion and Public Life* found that 49 percent of Pentecostals do not speak in tongues. Unless the waters flow, our churches cannot truly address the need of the human heart.

THE THRESHOLD

The threshold speaks of place and position. It speaks of the floor and denotes humility. The threshold typifies the person, who must get down on his knees spiritually speaking, and put his head down in order to drink the water. Pride is one of the major reasons people don't seek the infilling of the Holy Spirit.

THE ALTAR

The phrase, *"For the forefront of the house stood toward the east, and the waters came down from under from the right side of the house, at the south side of the altar,"* denotes the course of the river, the altar of Jehovah, i.e., Calvary. Let's say it this way: The course of this river is the Cross of Christ. The Holy Spirit comes through Calvary. Every grace and benefit we have comes to us through what Christ did at Calvary. I don't know what you desire, but I want that river to flow into my life, for everything the river touches shall live.

CHURCH, READ
—— THE ——
BOOK OF ACTS
—— AND ——
GET READY!

CHAPTER 19

SAUL WAS REFRESHED AND WELL

"BUT THE SPIRIT OF the LORD departed from Saul, and an evil spirit from the LORD troubled him. And Saul's servants said unto him, Behold now, an evil spirit from God troubles you. Let our lord now command your servants, which are before you, to seek out a man, who is a cunning player on an harp: and it shall come to pass, when the evil spirit from God is upon you, that he shall play with his hand, and you shall be well. And Saul said unto his servants, Provide me now a man who can play well, and bring him to me. Then answered one of the servants, and said, Behold, I have seen a son of Jesse the Beth-lehemite, who is cunning in playing, and a mighty valiant man, and a man of war, and prudent in matters, and a comely person, and the LORD is with him. Wherefore Saul sent messengers unto Jesse, and said, Send me David your son, which is with the sheep. And Jesse took an ass laden with bread, and a bottle of wine, and a kid, and sent them by David his son unto Saul. And David came to Saul, and stood before him: and he loved him greatly; and he became his armourbearer. And Saul sent to Jesse, saying, Let David, I pray you, stand before me; for he has found favour in my

sight. And it came to pass, when the evil spirit from God was upon Saul, that David took an harp, and played with his hand: so Saul was refreshed, and was well, and the evil spirit departed from him." (I Sam.16:14-23).

In this story we are given insight into the spirit world. There are two spirits at work in the world and the church— the Holy Spirit and evil spirits. That which is biblical is always accompanied by the Holy Spirit, and that which is unscriptural is backed by evil spirits.

The spirit world is never neutral, meaning that what you accept regarding spiritual matters will either lead you closer to the Lord or further away from the Lord. This is exactly what happened to Saul and to Israel. When they followed the Lord, they had the help of the Holy Spirit. When they departed from the Lord's prescribed path, they were at the mercy of demon spirits that brought heartache and misery.

When we read this story, we are reading some of the most sorrowful words in the Bible. David would refer to Saul's ultimate destruction with the words, *"How are the mighty fallen!"* (II Sam. 1:19).

APOSTASY

There is no debate on the fact that Saul led Israel astray; however, it must be understood that Israel's apostasy started before Saul became king. Apostasy in the church is never sudden; it is gradual. It always begins with God's people no longer walking in God's ways but walking after their own desires. We can see the beginning of Israel's apostasy in Chapter 8 of I Samuel. It says in Verses 1 and 2 that Samuel made his sons, Joel and Abiah, judges over Israel. Understand that Samuel was the prophet of God, the voice of God to the people, and a great man of God, yet, in placing his sons as judges, he failed the Lord. Verse 3 says, *"And his sons walked not in his ways, but turned aside."*

There are two spiritual truths contained here: First, even God's anointed make mistakes and miss the will of God. Second, heritage does not equal salvation or righteousness. Everyone must seek the Lord for direction, and everyone must have his own personal relationship with the Lord.

The text says of Samuel's sons that they were guilty of three sins:

1. They were after money.
2. They took bribes.
3. They perverted judgment.

Ungodly leadership in the church always takes from the people and never gives anything back.

ISRAEL'S DEMANDS

In looking at the evil of Samuel's sons, the people began to look at the nations that surrounded them, and they said to Samuel, *"Make us a king to judge us like all the nations"* (I Sam. 8:5).

Israel's twofold sin was:

1. Self-will—they wanted their way and not God's way.
2. They wanted to be like the pagan nations that surrounded them.

Self-will is the beginning of all of our problems. When the church or believers chart their own course, the end will result in becoming like the world.

They said, *"Make* (give) *us a king to judge us."* Though the Lord was planning to give them a king (David), they didn't want to operate in God's time. They no longer wanted God; they wanted a man.

TO REJECT GOD

To reject God's will and way is to reject God Himself. The Lord told Samuel, *"They have rejected Me"* (I Sam. 8:7). Take note of this and don't ever forget that when we go against God and His will and ways, we are rejecting Him, and the only thing left is Satan.

Notice here that Israel's problems started before Saul became king. Today in the church, when we look at all the foolishness and false doctrine in the church, we are quick to lay the blame at the feet of preachers, yet, the fact is, while that is a problem, the blame must also be placed at the feet of the laity. Paul said in II Timothy 4:3, *"For the time will come when they* (the people) *will not endure sound doctrine; but after their own lusts shall they heap to themselves teachers, having itching ears."*

So, now, because of the people's desires, they would get what they demanded, and it would turn out to be bad.

THE SPIRIT OF THE LORD
DEPARTED FROM SAUL

Saul eventually departed from God's way and went into rebellion, which the Lord called witchcraft. It was the downward spiral, with Saul gradually going deeper and deeper into sin. There are two truths contained in this statement:

1. Even though Saul was not God's choice, the Lord didn't just throw him aside, but He tried to work with him and use him. This is God's grace at work.
2. The Holy Spirit will not stay where He is not wanted. The more of the Spirit of God one desires, the more he will have. Jesus said in Matthew 5:6, *"Blessed are they which do hunger and thirst after righteousness for they shall be filled."* Yet, when the believer no longer hungers and thirsts after that which is of God, the Holy Spirit will depart.

THE MODERN CHURCH

In looking at the state of affairs in the modern Pentecostal denominations, I believe that if one is completely honest, he will have to admit that the Spirit of the Lord has departed from some churches. How can I say that? I can say that because the facts bear it out that fewer people are being saved and baptized with the Holy Spirit than ever before. The Spirit of the Lord has departed—sad, but true.

AN EVIL SPIRIT

The text says that *"An evil spirit from the LORD troubled him."* This doesn't literally mean that the Lord sent an evil spirit, but that He allowed it. As I stated earlier, when one rejects the Holy Spirit, one is left with evil spirits. This evil spirit troubled Saul. This speaks of emotional discord, mental turmoil, and an enraged spirit.

Satan operates two ways against mankind: One way is oppression, which manifests itself in depression, gloom, and melancholy. Oppression operates against both the saved and the unsaved. The other way is possession. Demonic possession is not possible for a believer. In spite of what some in the charismatic world may say, there is absolutely nothing in the Bible to suggest such a thing; however, every believer, at some time in his life, has to deal with satanic oppression.

THE CURE FOR DEMONIC OPPRESSION

The cure for this satanic attack is Jesus Christ and Him crucified (Rom. 6:1-14; 8:1-12, 11; I Cor. 1:17-18, 21, 23; 2:2; Gal., Chpt. 5; 6:14; Col. 2:14-15). The Cross is the only answer for demon oppression. One's understanding of what Christ did at Calvary and one's faith in that finished work then allows the Holy Spirit to do His work, which we shall see in the rest of the text.

DAVID TOOK A HARP, AND PLAYED

This is the first mention of God's use of music for worship, refreshing, and healing, but we must understand that though David was talented, it was not his talent that brought relief; it was the anointing of the Holy Spirit.

SAUL WAS REFRESHED, AND WAS WELL

The power of darkness cannot stand in the presence of the Holy Spirit. Only the Holy Spirit brings rest, refreshing, and healing to the heart.

I hope you can get the picture: Saul, driven by demon spirits, would go into fits of anger and turmoil, but when the Spirit of God began to move, God's Spirit drove away the demon spirits.

The answer for you and your turmoil is to be in a place where the Holy Spirit can move. Where is that place? It is anywhere. The location is not important. The Holy Spirit works strictly within the confines of Calvary and when you go to the Cross, you are allowing the Holy Spirit to work on your behalf.

CHURCH, READ
—— THE ——
BOOK OF ACTS
—— AND ——
GET READY!

CHAPTER 20

THESE MEN DO EXCEEDINGLY TROUBLE OUR CITY

"*AND IT CAME TO pass, as we went to prayer, a certain damsel possessed with a spirit of divination met us, which brought her masters much gain by soothsaying: The same followed Paul and us, and cried, saying, These men are the servants of the Most High God, which show unto us the way of salvation. And this did she many days. But Paul, being grieved, turned and said to the spirit, I command you in the name of Jesus Christ to come out of her. And he came out the same hour. And when her masters saw that the hope of their gains was gone, they caught Paul and Silas, and drew them into the marketplace unto the rulers, and brought them to the magistrates, saying, These men, being Jews, do exceedingly trouble our city*" (Acts 16:16-20).

The mission of the church is not to seek peace or compromise with Satan's kingdom, but our mission is to trouble the kingdom of darkness. Jesus said in Matthew 5:14, "*You are the light of the world. A city that is set on an hill cannot be hid.*"

Through the power and anointing of the Holy Spirit, we are to shine brightly, pointing souls to Calvary, and have authority over demon spirits.

A CERTAIN DAMSEL POSSESSED
WITH A SPIRIT OF DIVINATION

This statement tells us that this poor girl was demon possessed. It speaks of the spirit of Python or Apollo. Python was, according to fable, a huge serpent that had an oracle on Mount Parnassus, famous for predicting future events.

Apollo was supposed to have slain this serpent and was thereafter called Pythius, becoming famous as the foreteller of future events. Simply put, it is a fortune-teller.

It was believed that all who pretended to foretell events were influenced by the spirit of Apollo Pythius.

WHICH BROUGHT HER MASTERS
MUCH GAIN BY SOOTHSAYING

In the Greek, this statement pertains to ventriloquism.

Evidently this spirit spoke through the girl by using a voice other than hers that claimed to give counsel, which in turn brought her masters a lot of money.

Many types of fortune-telling, astrology, and spiritism were common in the ancient pagan religions of that part of the world. Isaiah 47:12-14 refers to these things as part of pagan Babylon.

As mentioned, all of these things have their place in Satan's evil kingdom. As such, no believer should have anything to do with astrology, horoscopes, tarot cards, or anything of such ilk.

As Christians, we receive our guidance by the Holy Spirit, who always guides us according to the Word of God.

"The same followed Paul and us, and cried, saying, These men are the servants of the most high God, which show unto us the way of salvation" (Acts 16:17).

This statement implies that this commotion went on for some time. It seems that everywhere Paul went, this girl followed and created a great scene.

The phrase, *"These men are the servants of the most high God,"* did not mean the same thing to the Greeks and Romans as it would to Christians. To the Greeks or Romans, they would have assumed she was referring to one of their false gods, such as Zeus or Jupiter.

"Which show unto us the way of salvation." This statement should have been translated *"a way of salvation"* because the word in the Greek has no definite article. It reads *"a way,"* rather than *"the way,"* and should have been translated so.

DECEPTION

Satan was using this tactic to deceive the people, making it seem that Paul was presenting just another god among many gods worshipped in that day. Satan's greatest weapon is deception. He tries to make people think that Jesus Christ, Allah, Buddha, and any other false god are all the same and lead people to the same place. Just choose the one you are most comfortable with, for all roads lead to heaven.

PAUL, BEING GRIEVED

This phrase refers to Paul being angry with Satan for abusing this poor girl, and Paul was hurting for the girl and her terrible plight.

It is time the church got angry about what Satan is doing in the world today. The mantra of most of the church world today is for a "positive message" and a positive message only. However, I remind you of the anger of Christ when he cleansed the temple. There is a place for righteous anger. The church must become angry over Satan's wiles and angry over false doctrine that is leading the church astray.

THE ANSWER FOR DEMON SPIRITS

"I command you in the name of Jesus Christ to come out of her." This is the answer to Satan and his evil bondages—the name of Jesus Christ. There is power and authority in that precious name. Jesus Christ is greater than demon spirits, drug or alcohol addiction, homosexuality, or sickness.

AND HE CAME OUT THE SAME HOUR

This statement says it all. The work of Christ is instantaneous. *"If the Son therefore shall make you free, you shall be free indeed"* (Jn. 8:36). Jesus Christ doesn't offer Celebrate Recovery or any other 12-step program. He sets people free immediately.

THESE MEN DO EXCEEDINGLY TROUBLE OUR CITY

What a compliment! Every believer should be a trouble-maker in Satan's kingdom. Every believer should boldly stand up for Christ no matter what people think. So, today, begin to exercise your authority in Christ and trouble Satan's kingdom!

CHURCH, READ
—— THE ——
BOOK OF ACTS
—— AND ——
GET READY!

CHAPTER 21

THE RIVER

"*GOD IS OUR REFUGE and strength, a very present help in trouble. Therefore will not we fear, though the earth be removed, and though the mountains be carried into the midst of the sea; though the waters thereof roar and be troubled, though the mountains shake with the swelling thereof. Selah. There is a river, the streams whereof shall make glad the city of God, the holy place of the tabernacles of the most High*" (Ps. 46:1-4).

We do not know who actually wrote this psalm or the specific time of its writing; however, some scholars believe that it is possible that it was written by the prophet Isaiah during the siege of Jerusalem by the Assyrians (II Chronicles, Chapter 23; II Kings, Chapter 18; Isaiah, Chapters 36-39). If that is so, then, no doubt, the Holy Spirit gave this to Isaiah in order that it be given to Hezekiah at Jerusalem.

If it were written today, it would have a double meaning:

1. God addressed Himself to the siege of Jerusalem by Sennacherib; and

2. Even more so, it pertains to the siege of Jerusalem by the Antichrist (Zech. 14:1-13) when the Lord will defend Jerusalem and defeat the Antichrist in a great victory.

At that future day, God will be Israel's only refuge and also a very present help.

However, I want to deal with the meaning these verses have for us today. I want to begin not with the beginning of Psalm 46:1, but rather with the last word of that verse.

TROUBLE

Just as Israel faced great trouble during Sennacherib's siege of Jerusalem, and just as Israel will face great trouble during the time of the Antichrist, so, too, do we as believers face trouble in our own lives. In the Hebrew the word *trouble* means "distress, a situation of extreme discomfort, affliction, or anguish."

There is no such thing as a life of ease and comfort as a believer, though we can have peace in the midst of trouble. Still, trouble and affliction are going to come our way. We are in a system of the world that is ruled by demon spirits that war against the child of God (Eph. 6:12). Peter addressed this in I Peter 4:12: *"Beloved, think it not strange concerning the fiery trial which is to try you, as though some strange thing happened unto you."*

We are in a spiritual war, and Satan is not going to let up. His attacks cover every aspect of one's life and living— spiritual, physical, financial, emotional, and domestical.

Not only do we have to contend with Satan and his minions, but let's face it, our biggest problem is us. We make foolish decisions; we listen to people with their bad advice. We don't seek the Lord, and we let our flesh rule, but believe me, the flesh must be fed, and it's never good.

The Lord also allows trouble to come our way to teach us dependence, trust, and faith, and even more so to teach us how fallible we are. Deuteronomy 8:2 says: *"And you shall remember all the way which the* LORD *your God led you … and to prove you, to know what was in your heart, whether you would keep His commandments, or no."*

As the notes in The Expositor's Study Bible say regarding this verse: "With the believer, everything is a test. How will we act? How will we react?"

So, the trouble is going to come, yet we have this promise.

REFUGE

The text begins with the heart-stirring promise, *"God is our refuge."* The Hebrew for God is, of course, *Elohim* and as it is used here, it conveys to us that God is the Creator, the King, the Judge, the Lord, and the Saviour. He is everything we need.

The word *refuge* means a "place of safety and protection, security, and a place of hope." He is the one; we are to run to Him, and we are to place our trust in Him. His refuge is complete and secure. His refuge provides for us everything we need during the time of trouble.

STRENGTH

Verse 1 says that not only is the Lord our refuge, but He is also our strength. *Strength* in the Hebrew means "power and might," and the greatest expression of His power and might was His victory over Satan on Calvary's Cross and His glorious resurrection.

A VERY PRESENT HELP

This tells us that the Lord is our help *now*. He is a *now* God:

- His power is *now*.
- His grace is *now*.
- His joy is *now*.
- His healing is *now*.
- His miracles are *now*.

And He is the same yesterday, today, and forever (Heb. 13:8).

WE WILL NOT FEAR

Fear plagues all of us at times; however, we need not fear, for the Lord is working for us, fighting for us, providing for us, and interceding for us.

THE RIVER OF GOD

Psalm 46:4 begins with, *"There is a river."* This river is the river of God. It refers to the great river that will flow out from under the sanctuary in the coming kingdom age. It will grow larger as it goes, with one part going into the Dead Sea, and it will bring life to that which was once dead. The moment the river touches the Dead Sea, it will be filled with fish.

The river is a type of the Holy Spirit, of which water represents the Holy Spirit as life. This is life that is beyond anything you can imagine. The only true life there is, is the life which flows from the Holy Spirit. The river will sustain you, the river will bring joy and gladness of heart, and the river can take that which is barren and bring forth life.

The river—the Holy Spirit—is the strength and power of the believer and the church. We must get into the river, and we must let the river get into us, for that is where we find true life.

CHURCH, READ
THE
BOOK OF ACTS
AND
GET READY!

CHAPTER 22

WHAT ABOUT THE WIND
AND THE FIRE?

"AND WHEN THE DAY of Pentecost was fully come (the Feast of Pentecost, one of the seven great feasts ordained by God and practiced by Israel yearly; it took place fifty days after the Passover), *they were all with one accord in one place* (not the upper room where they had been previously meeting, but rather the temple [Lk. 24:53; Acts 2:46]). *And suddenly there came a sound from heaven as of a rushing mighty wind* (portrays the coming of the Holy Spirit in a new dimension, all made possible by the Cross), *and it filled all the house* (the temple) *where they were sitting* (they were probably in the court of the Gentiles). *And there appeared unto them cloven tongues like as of fire* (the only record of such in the New Testament, and was the fulfillment of the prophecy of John the Baptist concerning Jesus [Mat. 3:11]), *and it sat upon each of them* (refers to all who were there, not just the twelve apostles; the exact number is not known). *And they were all filled with the Holy Spirit* (all were filled, not just the apostles; due to the Cross, the Holy Spirit could now come into the hearts and lives of all believers to abide permanently [Jn. 14:16]), *and began to speak with other tongues* (the initial physical evidence that

one has been baptized with the Spirit, and was predicted by the prophet Isaiah [Isa. 28:9-12] and by Christ [Mk. 16:17; Jn. 15:26; 16:13]), *as the Spirit gave them utterance* (meaning they did not initiate this themselves, but that it was initiated by the Spirit; as we shall see, these were languages known somewhere in the world, but not by the speaker)" (Acts 2:1-4) (The Expositor's Study Bible).

As one can imagine, we receive questions about the Bible and doctrine from literally all over the world.

Without fail, questions about the Holy Spirit and the Acts, Chapter 2, experience are among the majority.

Many non-Pentecostal believers, who are opposed to speaking in tongues, and those who are curious, by and large ask many of the same questions. As an example, I will give you three of the questions we are asked most often and our answers:

1. Q: In I Corinthians, Chapter 14, isn't the apostle Paul telling us that tongues are not that important and is actually forbidding to speak in tongues during a service?

   A: No, that's not what he is saying. First of all, one must look at the context of the entire chapter. Paul himself states in Verse 18, *"I thank my God, I speak with tongues more than you all,"* and in Verse 39 he says, *"Forbid not to speak with tongues."* To understand what Paul is truly telling us, one must understand that Paul is dealing with order in a local assembly and regulating the vocal gifts of tongues, interpretation of tongues, and prophecy. He is not dealing with tongues as one's prayer language. He is telling us that it does the body no good for a message in tongues to be given if there is no one there to interpret. He is saying that in the case of no interpretation, prophecy would serve the body better as everyone would understand what is said. I get emails all the time from non-Pentecostals who are watching me preach, and as the Lord starts moving, I will praise Him in my prayer language. They say, "You were out of order because it was not interpreted." I write them back and tell them, "No, I was not out of order." Why? Because I was not giving a message in tongues; I was just praising the Lord. Everyone who is filled with the Spirit will speak in tongues, but not everyone who speaks in tongues has the gift of tongues, one of the nine gifts of the Spirit.

2. Q: Do I need to speak in tongues to go to heaven?

A: No. Salvation is by faith through grace, and it is afforded to everyone who repents and asks Christ into their hearts. To add the requirement of tongues is to nullify grace and add works to the process.

3. Q: You Pentecostals say you are continuing the Acts 2

experience and that it is for today, so why don't we feel the mighty rushing wind and see the tongues of fire?

A: Since this is the question we probably receive most often, allow me the remainder of this chapter to answer it. On the day of Pentecost, two important and outstanding events took place:

1. The Holy Spirit was *given*. On the day of Pentecost, the Holy Spirit was given. The evidence of the Spirit being given was the wind and the fire. Both were the announcement that now the Holy Spirit could be given to man in a way that was not possible in the old covenant. The wind and fire signified His presence now given on a once-and-for-all basis. There is no need today for us to see the fire or feel the wind, for on Pentecost He came, and He has never left. Praise God the Holy Spirit has been in our midst and in the hearts of untold millions for nearly 2,000 years. He is here, and He's not leaving.

2. The Holy Spirit was *received*. The second great event to happen on the day of Pentecost was the Holy Spirit, who was given, was then received, with the evidence—believers speaking in tongues.

The first event—the Holy Spirit *given*—was a specific act at a specific time for all believers of every generation, and it was never to be repeated. However, the Holy Spirit being *received* happened not only then, but also now, and until the end of all ages for all who will believe. Only one time in the book of Acts is the wind and fire mentioned, and that was when He was given, but there are several instances in the book of Acts where tongues are mentioned as it regards believers being filled (Acts, Chpts. 2, 9-10, 19). As well, in Acts, Chapter 8, regarding Peter and John in Samaria, while tongues are not mentioned, Verse 21 says, concerning Simon the sorcerer, *"You have neither part nor lot in this matter."* The word *matter* in the Greek, as is used here, is *logos* and means "a word or speech." So, Peter actually said, "You have neither part nor lot in this utterance." It is clear that he was speaking of tongues.

Thank God, the Holy Spirit was given, and thank God, I have received Him.

CHURCH, READ
—— THE ——
BOOK OF ACTS
——AND——
GET READY!

CHAPTER 23

THE FUNCTION OF
THE HOLY SPIRIT

"*IN THE BEGINNING* (refers to the beginning of creation, or at least the creation as it refers to this universe; God, unformed, unmade, uncreated, had no beginning; He always was, always is, and always shall be) *God* (the phrase, 'In the beginning God,' explains the first cause of all things as it regards creation) *created the heaven and the earth* (could be translated 'the heavens and the earth' because God created the entirety of the universe). *And the earth was without form, and void; and darkness was upon the face of the deep* (God did not originally create the earth without form and void; it became this way after a cataclysmic happening; this happening was the revolt of Lucifer against God, which took place sometime in the dateless past). *And the Spirit of God* (Holy Spirit) *moved upon the face of the waters* (the moving of the Holy Spirit signified and signifies the beginning of life)" (Gen. 1:1-2) (The Expositor's Study Bible).

It has been said that the moving of the Holy Spirit is the first sign of life. As it regards our born-again experience, everything is evidence of that great truth.

We were all born into sin and darkness, but the Holy Spirit moved and brought the light of Jesus Christ into our lives.

THE CREATION STORY

Genesis 1:1-2 gives to us much more information than just the creation of the world, but, as well, we see how the Holy Spirit functions in the world, the church, and in the lives of all believers if they truly allow Him to have His way.

OPERATION

Genesis 1:2, *"The earth was without form, and void"* of life, but then the text says, *"The Spirit of God moved."* When the Spirit moved, that which was of no form and void of life immediately changed. Order came out of chaos and light out of darkness. The Holy Spirit in His operation brought change. This is what the Holy Spirit desires in our churches and in our lives. He wants to operate, He wants to move, and He wants to bring life, faith, power, and victory.

If the Holy Spirit is not allowed to have His way in our churches, then there is no reason to have church, for His operation changes lives, heals the sick, mends the brokenhearted, and satisfies man's heart.

ILLUMINATION

Genesis 1:3 says, *"And God said, Let there be light: and*

there was light." It is the job of the Holy Spirit to bring illumination to our lives. He illuminates truth, He gives guidance, and He shows us the right path by illuminating Jesus Christ. His job is to shine the light of truth upon Christ.

SEPARATION

Genesis 1:4 says, *"God divided the light from the darkness."* It is the function of the Holy Spirit to bring about separation from the world and from self.

It is a complete and total way of life. Darkness speaks of sin and error while light speaks of righteousness and truth, who is Jesus Christ. We are to be separated unto Him and Him alone.

CREATION

Genesis 1:21 tells us that God, through the Holy Spirit, created the animal kingdom. The Holy Spirit creates a new life in us. He creates us from death, and a new man is brought forth. He creates something out of nothing; He creates order out of chaos, life out of death, and prosperity out of poverty. The Holy Spirit creates.

MULTIPLICATION

Genesis 1:28 says of earth's first inhabitants, *"And God blessed them, and God said unto them, Be fruitful, and multiply."* He gives us more. He multiplies to us more than we could ever hope for: Justification, sanctification, and blessings from above. He multiplies the bread and fish to feed a multitude. When the disciples had fished all night and caught nothing, He said, *"Launch out into the deep, and let down your nets for a draught* (catch)*"* (Lk. 5:4). Where there had been no fish, He multiplied the catch so that it not only filled up Peter's boat but also the boat that belonged to James and John. The Holy Spirit wants to multiply in our lives that which we need.

The Holy Spirit moved; let Him move in you and through you. Let Him move in our churches as in days of old. Let Him operate, let Him illuminate, let Him separate, let Him create, and let Him multiply your loaves and fishes.

CHURCH, READ
——THE——
BOOK OF ACTS
——AND——
GET READY!

CHAPTER 24

SEVEN STEPS TO RECEIVING
THE HOLY SPIRIT

"WHEREFORE, BRETHREN, COVET TO prophesy (desire the gift of prophecy), *and forbid not to speak with tongues.* (This proclaims the fact that all the instructions he has given are not meant to disallow tongues, but rather to put them in their rightful order. So where does that put the so-called religious leaders who ignore this particular statement, which is actually a 'commandment of the Lord'?)" (I Cor. 14:39) (The Expositor's Study Bible).

There is much confusion among non-Pentecostals regarding I Corinthians, Chapter 14. Paul wrote this chapter to regulate and give instruction as it regarded three spiritual gifts: prophecy, tongues, and interpretation of tongues, which are called the vocal gifts—three of the nine gifts of the Spirit.

Next are the three revelation gifts: word of wisdom, the word of knowledge, and the discerning of spirits.

Last are the three power gifts: the gift of faith, the gift of healing, and the gift of the working of miracles.

There is a difference in the gift of tongues and the tongues one receives at the moment of his infilling. All who are filled with the Spirit baptism will speak in tongues, but not all who speak in tongues have the gift of tongues. Likewise, one who has the gift of prophecy is not necessarily a prophet.

There was no regulation or order given to the early church regarding tongues and interpretation of tongues. The gist of Paul's command is very simple: A message in tongues does the church no good if there is no one to interpret it. Therefore, Paul states that if a prophecy is given, then the body, as all in attendance, would be able to understand it. He is by no means denigrating or dismissing tongues, as the chapter will clearly bear out.

SPEAKS UNTO GOD

In I Corinthians 14:2 the Bible says, *"For he who speaks in an unknown tongue speaks not unto men, but unto God: for no man understands him; howbeit in the Spirit he speaks mysteries."*

The phrase, *"For he who speaks in an unknown tongue speaks not unto men, but unto God,"* tells us the following:

1. The word *unknown* was supplied by the translators, as it was not in the original text. It actually means that it is unknown to the speaker and most of the time to the listeners, as well, but not unknown as far as language is concerned. Tongues are always a language known somewhere in the world. It is not babble or gibberish as some detractors say. There are many languages.

Actually, the Bible has been translated into 2,179 different languages, but there are many more than that spoken in the world. Linguists state that there are 6,809 distinct languages.

2. The term, *"Speaks not unto men,"* means that if the Lord is speaking to men, He will speak to them in the language they understand. Tongues are not meant to be understood by men unless it is intended by the Holy Spirit to be interpreted.

3. The phrase, *"But unto God,"* is meant to say that one can speak in tongues silently in praise and worship because it is only to God to whom one is speaking. The phrase, *"Howbeit in the Spirit he speaks mysteries,"* is to be understood in this fashion: *Mysteries* in the Greek is *musterion* and means "a secret." It's a secret between God and man.

THE BIBLE EVIDENCE OF THE BAPTISM WITH THE HOLY SPIRIT

There are five recorded instances of people receiving the Holy Spirit in the book of Acts. They are: Acts 2:1-16, Acts 8:14-18, Acts 9:17, and Acts 10:44-46.

The verses given record the five instances of people being filled. They covered a period of about 20 years and involved from one to many individuals. Three times out of the five it is recorded that they spoke with tongues, and the other two instances imply that they spoke with tongues.

Paul himself said in I Corinthians 14:18, *"I thank my God, I speak with tongues more than you all."*

IS IT NECESSARY TO SPEAK IN TONGUES?

For salvation, no, it is not necessary to speak in tongues, but if one wants the true New Testament experience, then one should want to speak with other tongues exactly as the Bible says. Don't make the mistake of seeking tongues. We don't seek tongues; we seek the infilling of the Holy Spirit, with tongues being the initial physical evidence one has been filled.

SEVEN STEPS TO RECEIVING THE INFILLING OF THE HOLY SPIRIT

1. You must be born again. There is only one requirement for one to be baptized with the Holy Spirit, and that is to be saved. No other requirements are needed. Salvation now prepares one for the Holy Spirit to come and live and work in a new and dynamic fashion.

2. You must decide that it is scriptural. You must settle it in your spirit once and for all that this great gift is for all believers for all time. There must not be any doubt in your heart. Don't let Satan fill your mind with all kinds of negative thoughts. Don't let those who are not believers of the Spirit baptism influence you negatively.

3. You must have faith. Everything we receive from the Lord is always by faith. We are to believe what He has promised in His Word, and He has most certainly promised the Holy Spirit (Acts 1:4; Joel 2:28-29; Isa. 28:11-12). Hebrews 11:6 says, *"Without faith it is impossible to please Him: for he that comes to God must believe that He is, and that He is a rewarder of them who diligently seek Him."*

4. You must not fear. Don't be afraid of opening yourself up to the spirit world, fearing that something of Satan will come upon you. Luke 11:11-13 says: *"If a son shall ask bread of any of you that is a father, will he give him a stone? or if he ask a fish, will he for a fish give him a serpent? Or if he shall ask an egg, will he offer him a scorpion? If you then, being evil, know how to give good gifts unto your children: how much more shall your heavenly Father give the Holy Spirit to them who ask Him?"*

5. Expect. You are to expect the Holy Spirit to put supernatural words (tongues) into your spirit and then for the Holy Spirit to move upon your vocal organs. The Lord will not force you to speak in tongues. He will give the utterance, but we have to speak.

6. Yield. By yielding I am meaning that in your heart you should say to the Lord, "I am asking You, Lord, to fill me with the Holy Spirit, and by faith I now receive." We are not to beg, for the infilling of the Holy Spirit is a free gift; neither are we to continue to pray out loud

in our own tongue because one cannot speak in two languages at once.

7. Receive. You must understand that God has already given the Spirit and that it is a gift; consequently, the only thing one is to do respecting a gift is to receive it. So, you must say, "I am going to receive this gift of God."

So, now, if you haven't received, then go through these steps and by faith receive.

CHURCH, READ
——— THE ———
BOOK OF ACTS
——— AND ———
GET READY!

CHAPTER 25

I WILL POUR WATER UPON HIM WHO IS THIRSTY

"FOR I WILL POUR water upon him who is thirsty, and floods upon the dry ground: I will pour My Spirit upon your seed, and My blessing upon your offspring (this promise had a fulfillment at Pentecost; but the future only will bring the total fulfillment. The 'water' here is a figure of the Holy Spirit; the 'willows,' a figure of the sons of Israel. This is the promise to which Peter pointed in Acts 2:39. It is a promise to Israel and to her children. As such, and as other Scriptures show, it was to overflow from Israel to all the nations of the earth. It will yet do so!): *And they shall spring up as among the grass, as willows by the water courses.* (Israel rejected their 'Pentecost' some 2,000 years ago. But now at the second advent of Christ, they will accept, and gladly! At this time, He will 'pour water upon him who is thirsty and floods upon the dry ground.' This infusion of the Holy Spirit upon and within Israel shall cause them to blossom as 'willows by the water courses.')" (Isa. 44:3-4) (The Expositor's Study Bible).

The literal meaning of this passage refers to Israel during the kingdom age when the Holy Spirit, symbolized by the use of the word *water*, will be poured out, and blessings unparalleled will rain upon Israel. However, the spirit of the text can definitely apply to us today, which is what I am dealing with in this chapter.

THE HOLY SPIRIT, GOD'S GREATEST GIFT TO THE CHURCH

As salvation is God's greatest gift to the world, the mighty infilling of the Holy Spirit with the evidence of speaking in tongues is God's greatest gift to the church. Everything done in the church and in our lives today is done through the person, office, and work of the Holy Spirit.

As well, during the ministry of Christ, everything He did was as a man filled with the Holy Spirit (Lk. 4:16-19), and if Christ had to have the Holy Spirit, how much more do we who are flawed and frail need the Holy Spirit?

I WILL POUR WATER UPON HIM WHO IS THIRSTY

There is a thirst in man that cannot be satisfied outside of the person and indwelling of the Holy Spirit. Religion cannot satisfy that thirst, and the world cannot satisfy that thirst.

In John 14:16-18, Jesus said, *"And I will pray the Father, and He shall give you another Comforter, that He may abide with you forever; Even the Spirit of truth; whom the world cannot receive, because it sees Him not, neither knows Him: but you know Him; for He dwells with you, and shall be in you. I will not leave you comfortless: I will come to you."*

Water, a symbol of the Holy Spirit, speaks of life. Just as the ground must have water for crops to grow, and just as the physical body must have water to live, spiritual man must have the living water of the Holy Spirit flowing in his life.

Notice that the Lord said, *"I will,"* an emphatic statement meaning that nothing can stop Him from doing what He says He is going to do. Likewise, nothing can stop us from receiving, except ourselves, whether through lack of faith or lack of yielding. Satan cannot stop the outpouring of the Holy Spirit upon those who hunger and thirst after righteousness.

The word *pour* means "to overflow." This tells us that what the Holy Spirit desires is to overflow us, saturate us, and literally consume us in the water of the Holy Spirit.

AND FLOODS UPON THE DRY GROUND

The world and religion are dry ground, parched and starved, but there are floods of living water available to us. The Holy Spirit through Ezekiel describes the Holy Spirit as a flowing river (Ezek. 47:5). He then said, *"And everything shall live whither the river comes"* (Ezek. 47:9). When the Holy Spirit begins to flow, the dry ground becomes a veritable ground of life and harvest.

I WILL POUR MY SPIRIT UPON YOUR SEED, AND MY BLESSING UPON YOUR OFFSPRING

Israel is seed, but we who are Gentiles who have accepted Christ are now His offspring, and He has promised to pour out His Spirit upon us. This brings blessing not only to us, but to our offspring as well.

AND THEY SHALL SPRING UP AS AMONG THE GRASS, AS WILLOWS BY THE WATER COURSES

Willows refers to a certain type of tree that will grow only near flowing water. The Holy Spirit will make you strong as a tree, spiritually speaking. Let the river flow right where you are. Open your heart to Him and by faith, receive the blessed Holy Spirit, and you will begin to sing:

There's a river of life flowing out from me,
Makes the lame to walk and the blind to see,
Opens prison doors, sets the captives free,
There's a river of life flowing out from me.

Spring up a well within my soul,
Spring up a well and make me whole,
Spring up a well and give to me,
That life abundantly.

I'll close this chapter with the same verse I opened with from Isaiah 44:3: *"I will pour water upon him who is thirsty."*

CHURCH, READ
—THE—
BOOK OF ACTS
—AND—
GET READY!

CHAPTER 26

THE DAY OF PENTECOST

"**AND WHEN THE DAY** of *Pentecost was fully come* (the Feast of Pentecost, one of the seven great feasts ordained by God and practiced by Israel yearly; it took place fifty days after Passover), *they were all with one accord in one place* (not the upper room where they had been previously meeting, but rather the temple [Lk. 24:53; Acts 2:46]). *And suddenly there came a sound from heaven as of a rushing mighty wind* (portrays the coming of the Holy Spirit in a new dimension, all made possible by the Cross), *and it filled all the house* (the temple) *where they were sitting* (they were probably in the court of the Gentiles). *And there appeared unto them cloven tongues like as of fire* (the only record of such in the New Testament, and was the fulfillment of the prophecy of John the Baptist concerning Jesus [Mat. 3:11]), *and it sat upon each of them* (refers to all who were there, not just the twelve apostles; the exact number is not known). *And they were all filled with the Holy Spirit* (all were filled, not just the apostles; due to the Cross, the Holy Spirit could now come into the hearts and lives of all believers to abide permanently [Jn. 14:16]), *and began* *to speak with other tongues* (the initial physical evidence that one has been baptized with the Spirit, and was predicted by the prophet Isaiah [Isa. 28:9-12], and by Christ [Mk. 16:17; Jn. 15:26; 16:13]), *as the Spirit gave them utterance* (meaning they did not initiate this themselves, but that it was initiated by the Spirit; as we shall see, these were languages known somewhere in the world, but not by the speaker)" (Acts 2:1-4) (The Expositor's Study Bible).

This chapter is actually from a sermon I preached about 18 years ago. I recently came across it while looking through some of my old preaching Bibles, and as I looked over the notes, it blessed me to the point that I thought it would make a great addition to this book, so I hope you enjoy and learn from it.

THE INFILLING OF THE HOLY SPIRIT IS NOT AN OPTION BUT A COMMAND

In Acts, Chapter 1, which could be called the last will and testament of the Lord Jesus Christ, the Lord gave the following instructions just prior to His ascension to the Father in heaven:

1. He *"commanded them that they should not depart from Jerusalem, but wait for the promise of the Father, which, said He, you have heard of Me"* (Acts 1:4).

2. *"For John truly baptized with water; but you shall*

be baptized with the Holy Spirit not many days hence" (Acts 1:5).

3. Then, in Acts 1:8, our Lord said, *"But you shall receive power, after that the Holy Spirit is come upon you: and you shall be witnesses unto Me both in Jerusalem, and in all Judaea, and in Samaria, and unto the uttermost part of the earth."*

So, one can see the importance the Lord placed upon His followers being filled with the Holy Spirit. Therefore, if the Lord would use His last words to His followers to be filled with the Holy Spirit, then we today should take heed to His command.

THE DAY OF PENTECOST

The day of Pentecost refers to the Feast of Pentecost, which was one of the seven feasts Israel was to observe. *Pentecost* means "fiftieth," and that feast occurred 50 days after the Feast of Passover.

It's interesting to note that on the very first Pentecost observed, which was in the wilderness 50 days after the first Passover in Egypt, the Bible says that 3,000 men of Israel were killed due to Israel's sin with the golden calf. The second chapter of the book of Acts records that on the day of Pentecost, 3,000 men were saved.

In this chapter, I want to deal with specific words or phrases that give us a greater insight into the person and the work of the Holy Spirit. So, let's look at them now.

ONE ACCORD

This phrase *"one accord"* means "to be like-minded." The idea is that it is the desire and work of the Holy Spirit in our lives to bring us into like-mindedness with the Lord and His Word. He desires to form us into the image of Christ in word and deed. The Holy Spirit is always in perfect agreement with Christ and His Word. A lot of religious bias and error would fall to the wayside if we would ask the Holy Spirit to help us understand the Bible.

SUDDENLY

As is used in Acts 2:2, the word *suddenly* means "an unexpected occurrence," as in you never know when the Holy Spirit is going to move. You don't have to be in church for there to be a sudden unexpected moving of the Holy Spirit in your heart. It can happen during your prayer time or during your Bible study. It can happen in service during the praise and worship. That's one of the most beautiful things about the Holy Spirit. While we might not know when He is going to move, He does, and when He does move, what a change He brings.

A SOUND FROM HEAVEN

The word *sound* means "something which is heard," or another meaning is "echo." The Holy Spirit desires to be heard in our hearts and our services. As well, as it regards the word *echo*, the idea is that if we let the Holy Spirit have His way in our lives, we become an echo of only what the Word of God has to say.

RUSHING MIGHTY WIND

Wind is one of the five symbols of the Holy Spirit, and it speaks of the power of the Holy Spirit. The mighty power of the Holy Spirit is greater than the forces of darkness that war against us. The power of the Spirit is what our churches need—power to see souls saved, sick bodies healed, believers filled with the Spirit, demons cast out, and broken hearts mended.

FILLED

This word *filled* means "to furnish." The idea is that the Holy Spirit is the one to furnish what we need, such as grace, anointing, faith, power, wisdom, guidance, etc. The word also means "to finish." Whatever the Lord starts, the Holy Spirit finishes (see Gen. 1:1-2). It also means "to dwell in." Jesus told His disciples that when the Holy Spirit would come, He would not only be with man, but He would dwell within man (Jn. 14:17).

CLOVEN

The word *cloven* means "to separate" or "to divide." The idea is that if we let the Holy Spirit have His way in our hearts, He will separate or divide us from that which is false and not of God.

FIRE

Fire is another symbol of the Holy Spirit, and it speaks of

purity. In Matthew 3:11-12, John the Baptist said, *"I indeed baptize you with water unto repentance: but He who comes after me is mightier than I, whose shoes I am not worthy to bear: He shall baptize you with the Holy Spirit, and with fire: Whose fan is in His hand, and He will thoroughly purge His floor, and gather His wheat into the garner; but He will burn up the chaff with unquenchable fire."* The idea is that even though one is saved and even filled with the Holy Spirit, there are still things in our lives that are not pleasing to the Lord that He wants to purge out of our lives.

This is not automatic. It is something one must desire and seek for the Lord to show us what must be purified in our lives.

SAT

The word *sat* means "to hover over." The idea of this word is that the Holy Spirit not only dwells within us, but He also hovers over us. He saturates us. He covers us in His mighty power.

As a Spirit-filled believer, I desire for all of these attributes of the Holy Spirit to be prevalent in my life, and I hope you do too.

CHURCH, READ
THE
BOOK OF ACTS
AND
GET READY!

CHAPTER 27

THE ALTAR, THE LAMP, THE OIL

"AND YOU SHALL COMMAND the children of Israel, that they bring you pure oil olive beaten for the light, to cause the lamp to burn always. In the tabernacle of the congregation without the veil, which is before the testimony, Aaron and his sons shall order it from evening to morning before the LORD: *it shall be a statute forever unto their generations on the behalf of the children of Israel"* (Ex. 27:20-21).

The Lord has called SonLife Broadcasting Network to not only bring back to the church the Message of the Cross, but to also introduce the evangelical world to the great message of Pentecost. As well, we are called to reintroduce the Holy Spirit to those who call themselves Pentecostal but are Pentecostal in name only.

WHO IS THE HOLY SPIRIT?

Without the help, the leading, and the anointing of the Holy Spirit, the believer and the church will accomplish little for the Lord. All through the Bible we see the importance of the Holy Spirit. The text that serves as the basis of this article, which deals with the plans of the tabernacle, gives us a glimpse of the importance of the Holy Spirit.

The Holy Spirit is a person, a real being who thinks, acts, wills, feels, loves, speaks, and can be grieved. The Holy Spirit exhibits all the responses that identify one as a person. Though He cannot be seen by the natural eye, He definitely can be felt.

The Holy Spirit is also a deity; He is the third person of the Godhead—the Trinity. He is not one of three Gods or one-third of God, for God cannot be divided. God is one God (Deut. 6:4; I Jn. 5:7), yet He is externally self-existing in three distinct persons: the Father, the Son, and the Holy Spirit. Each of these three persons is fully God, yet, even though each is fully God, each is an individual person within Himself. The Father is God, Jesus is God, and the Holy Spirit is God.

MANY NAMES OF THE HOLY SPIRIT

Throughout Scripture, the Holy Spirit has revealed Himself by many different names. Some of those names are:

- the Spirit of God (I Cor. 3:16)
- the Spirit of His Son (Gal. 4:6)
- the Spirit of grace and of supplications (Zech. 12:10)
- the Spirit of wisdom and knowledge (Isa. 11:2)
- the Spirit of truth (Jn. 14:16-17)
- the Spirit of life (Rom. 8:2)
- the Comforter (Jn. 14:16)

SYMBOLS OF THE HOLY SPIRIT

There are five symbols given in God's Word that represent the varied works of the Holy Spirit.

They are:

1. The dove. This speaks of the gentleness and meekness of the Holy Spirit (Lk. 3:22).
2. Living water. This speaks of life. Just as the physical man must have water to live, so, too, must our spirit man have the living water of the Holy Spirit to live (Jn. 7:37-39).
3. Wind. This speaks of the power of the Holy Spirit (Acts 2:2).
4. Fire. This speaks of purity (Mat. 3:11).
5. Oil. This speaks of the anointing of the Holy Spirit and the illumination and light that shines upon Christ and His Word (James 5:14-16, Ex. 27:20-21).

THE TABERNACLE

Beginning with Exodus, Chapter 25, we find the instructions given to Moses for the tabernacle. Verse 1 of Chapter 27 begins with the words, *"And you shalt make an altar."*

THE ALTAR

The altar speaks of the Cross. Calvary is the foundation of Christianity. The Cross is not just another doctrine of the Bible, but it is the foundation by which all Bible doctrine flows.

The only way one can get to the Father is through the Son, and the only way to get to the Son is through Calvary.

Then, Verse 1 states, *"The altar shall be foursquare."* Each corner of the altar pointed north, south, east, and west, telling us that it is the same gospel for all of mankind, for all of humanity's problem is the same, and that is sin.

THE LAMPSTAND

In front of the altar was the golden lampstand. The golden lampstand was the only means of light in the tabernacle. Without the lampstand, the priests could not see properly to do their work.

THE OIL

Verse 20 states, *"You shall command the children of Israel, that they bring you pure oil olive, beaten for light."*

The oil was the fuel source for the golden lampstand, and as is obvious, this tells us that the Holy Spirit is the fuel source needed to bring illumination. Notice that the illumination of the light from the golden lampstand brought light upon the altar. The work of the Holy Spirit is to bring light to Jesus Christ.

In John 16:13 and 14, the Lord said: *"Howbeit when He, the Spirit of truth, is come, He will guide you into all truth: for He shall not speak of Himself; but whatsoever He shall hear, that shall He speak: and He will show you things to come. He shall glorify Me: for He shall receive of Mine, and shall show it unto you."*

As stated, the light generated by the Holy Spirit illuminated the altar or, in other words, the Cross. Without the help of the Holy Spirit, you will never be able to see the complete victory of the Cross. Without the oil, the church has no light but only darkness.

Twice a day Aaron and his sons were commanded to bring fresh oil to replenish the golden lampstand. This tells us that the oil of the Spirit in our lives is to be replenished daily. We can't live off past movings of the Holy Spirit. We must have the oil replenished every day of our lives.

Then, Verse 20 tells us *"to cause the lamp to burn always."* The light was never to go out; it was to burn 24 hours a day, seven days a week, 365 days a year.

Is your lamp burning brightly? Do you replenish the oil daily? We must have a never-ending source of oil flowing constantly.

The church needs the oil of the Holy Spirit as never before, and thanks be to God, the oil is available to any and all who will seek God for it.

CHURCH, READ
—— THE ——
BOOK OF ACTS
—— AND ——
GET READY!

CHAPTER 28

THE PRECIOUS BLOOD OF CHRIST

"FORASMUCH AS YOU KNOW that you were not redeemed with corruptible things, as silver and gold (presents the fact that the most precious commodities [silver and gold] could not redeem fallen man), *from your vain conversation* (vain lifestyle) *received by tradition from your fathers* (speaks of original sin that is passed on from father to child at conception); *But with the precious blood of Christ* (presents the payment, which proclaims the poured out life of Christ on behalf of sinners), *as of a lamb without blemish and without spot* (speaks of the lambs offered as substitutes in the old Jewish economy; the death of Christ was not an execution or assassination, but rather a sacrifice; the offering of Himself presented a perfect sacrifice, for He was perfect in every respect [Ex. 12:5])" (I Pet. 1:18-19) (The Expositor's Study Bible).

It is easy in ministry to fall into the habit of preaching about the gospel but to not preach the gospel itself. The gospel message is Christ, who He is—the Redeemer and Saviour—and what He did—died on the Cross for my sins as the only sacrifice that God the Father would accept.

REDEMPTION

In Verse 18 Peter states, *"Forasmuch as you know that you were not redeemed with corruptible things, as silver and gold."* This presents the fact that the work accomplished by Christ on Calvary was all of Him and none of us. We play no part except as it regards sin. Man in his guilt could not atone for man's sins; therefore, God became man—sinless, perfect, spotless, and blameless. He died in our place because He was sinless, and God accepted His death as a sacrifice, with His blood atoning for man's sins—past, present, and future.

The word *redeemed* means "to set free by the payment of ransom." This term refers to the buying of slaves in the slave market. By the use of this word, Peter clearly states that all before salvation were slaves to sin, Satan, passion, and self-will. No matter how educated fallen man may be, no matter how much money he may have, and no matter how cosmopolitan and sophisticated he may be, without Christ, he is a slave.

SILVER AND GOLD

The highest form of commerce that man values and for which man strives is silver and gold. However, no matter the worth of silver and gold, they are worthless when it comes to purchasing man's spiritual freedom. The value of a human soul is so great and so valuable as to defy all description. The soul of man is so valuable that there is nothing on earth that can redeem it.

Therefore, God had to become man in order that man could be bought back.

His death, with His body broken, was the only sacrifice God could accept. *"He ... who knew no sin,"* became sin (sin offering in the Greek), *"that we might be made the righteousness of God in Him"* (II Cor. 5:21).

VAIN CONVERSATION

This statement refers to our former lifestyle before conversion. *Vain* means "empty nothings." Solomon said, *"Vanity of vanities; all is vanity"* (Eccl. 1:2). Life is meaningless nothings without Christ.

TRADITION

The phrase, *"By tradition from your fathers,"* refers to the Mosaic law. Even though perfect and given by God to Moses, it was taken by man and perverted until it had become nothing but tradition. The law, even though from God, could not redeem man but only point out man's futile endeavors of perfection and good.

THE PRECIOUS BLOOD OF CHRIST

Now Peter tells us that the only thing that can redeem a slave of sin is the precious blood of Christ. *Precious* means "valuable, honored, costly." His blood, untainted by the fall, was pure, and it could do for man what silver, gold, tradition, and law could not do. His blood was the payment, which proclaims the poured out life of Christ, all on our behalf.

His poured out life was the only thing that could satisfy divine justice.

The blood of Christ is precious, valuable, costly, and honored because the blood of Jesus has done the following for all who will say yes to Him.

His blood is precious because:

- Through His blood we have God's atoning grace.
- His blood has washed away our sins.
- His blood has given us the promise and power of a redeemed, regenerated life.
- His blood has made us holy, righteous, and acceptable.
- His blood has justified and sanctified us.
- His blood brings healing to the mind, the soul, and the body.
- His blood frees us from the guilt of our past.
- His blood makes it possible for the Holy Spirit to live and dwell in man's heart.
- His blood has made us acceptable that we may now enter into the very presence of the throne of God.

Yes, my friend, the blood of Jesus Christ is the most precious substance in the world. As the songwriter wrote long ago:

> *What can wash away my sin?*
> *Nothing but the blood of Jesus.*
> *What can make me whole again?*
> *Nothing but the blood of Jesus.*

CHURCH, READ
—THE—
BOOK OF ACTS
—AND—
GET READY!

CHAPTER 29

AGAIN

"AGAIN THERE WAS A *day when the sons of God came to present themselves before the* LORD, *and Satan came also among them to present himself before the* LORD (regrettably, Satan always comes 'again'). *And the* LORD *said unto Satan, From where do you come? And Satan answered the* LORD, *and said, From going to and fro in the earth, and from walking up and down in it* (1:7). *And the* LORD *said unto Satan, Have you considered My servant Job, that there is none like him in the earth, a perfect and an upright man, one who fears God, and hates evil? and still he holds fast his integrity, although you moved Me against him, to destroy him without cause* (the Lord reminds Satan that Job did not do what Satan said he would do, which was to curse God [1:11]). *And Satan answered the* LORD, *and said, Skin for skin, yes, all that a man has will he give for his life* (while that is true for most, it definitely isn't true for all, even as it wasn't true for Job). *But put forth Your hand now, and touch his bone and his flesh, and he will curse You to Your face* (the trial deepens!). *And the* LORD *said unto Satan, Behold, he is in your hand; but save his life* (once again, the Lord sets the limits; Job's health can be affected, and severely so, but Satan cannot take his life; again we state: all of this shows that Satan can only do what the Lord allows him to do). *So went Satan forth from the presence of the LORD, and smote Job with sore boils from the sole of his foot unto his crown* (it is believed that this disease was 'elephantiasis,' which is a strongly developed form of leprosy; while it is a non-contagious disease, it is extremely painful, coming from burning and ulcerous swelling; generally, it attacks only a certain part of the body; however, Job was afflicted over the entirety of his body, which was not only notoriously painful but, as well, terribly humiliating, as would be obvious). *And he took him a potsherd to scrape himself withal; and he sat down among the ashes* (the sores, it is said, emit a fluid with an offensive odor; Job used the potsherd to scrape it away)" (Job 2:1-8) (The Expositor's Study Bible).

Job was the son of Issachar, the grandson of Jacob. It is believed by theologians that Moses wrote this book in collaboration with Job. It is believed that Moses was between 50 and 60 years of age and Job about 80 when the book was written. It is also believed that Job was the first book of the Bible to be written. If that is true, then Job is the oldest book in the world.

JOB'S THEME

The theme of the Bible is man's redemption through the sacrifice of God's son, Jesus Christ, on Calvary's Cross.

However, the theme of Job is not the conversion of a sinner, but the consecration of the saint. So, this great book deals with the believer's sanctification.

Job explains to us why bad things happen to good people. Bad things happen to bring us to a place of abhorrence of self and to dependence upon the Lord, to bring us to the place where we can say, *"Though He slay me, yet will I trust* (in) *Him"* (Job 13:15).

JUSTIFICATION AND SANCTIFICATION

In both Chapters 1 and 2 of the book of Job, the text says of Job that he was perfect and upright, and one who feared God. This by no means implies that Job was sinless, for the Bible does not teach sinless perfection in our present state, as Romans 3:23 clearly states, *"For all have sinned, and come short of the glory of God."* The statement as used in the text simply means that Job was doing all he could do to please God and to serve Him. In this we should understand the twin doctrines of justification and sanctification:

1. Justification is the act of God declaring one not guilty, innocent of all charges, and perfect as though the individual has never sinned. This is done upon the person's simple faith in Christ and His atoning sacrifice at Calvary.

2. Sanctification is different (as it comes first) in that at conversion, the believing sinner is instantly, totally,

and perfectly sanctified. In I Corinthians 6:11, Paul writes: *"And such were some of you: but you are washed, but you are sanctified, but you are justified in the name of the Lord Jesus, and by the Spirit of God."*

Sanctification is making one clean while justification is declaring one clean.

Sanctification is our position in Christ, which never changes; however, our condition in Christ does change according to our conduct, attitude, consecration, etc. It is the desire of the Holy Spirit to bring our condition up to our position. Though in God's eyes we are completely sanctified at conversion, the practical application of sanctification is progressive.

SATAN CAN ONLY DO WHAT GOD ALLOWS HIM TO DO!

In the first chapter of Job, we find Satan before the throne of God. We read that God engages Satan in a conversation about Job. As well, we see that the Lord allows Satan to come against Job, except for the taking of his life. This tells us that everything that happens to us as believers is either caused or allowed by God. While He never causes a Christian to sin, He definitely allows it.

So, in the space of one day, Job lost his wealth, his children, his servants, and his livestock. Reduced to poverty and brokenness, the Bible says, *"In all this Job sinned not, nor charged God foolishly"* (Job 1:22). Simply put, Job did not blame the Lord of Glory for his situation.

THE WORD *AGAIN* IN CHAPTER 2

The second chapter of Job begins with the word *again*: *"Again there was a day when the sons of God came to present themselves before the* LORD, *and Satan came also among them to present himself before the* LORD*"* (Job 2:1).

In this one word—*again*—there is a wealth of truth that we must all learn. This word tells us the following:

1. There is nothing the believer can do that will stop Satan from coming again and again to steal, kill, and destroy. I Peter 4:12 says, *"Beloved, think it not strange concerning the fiery trial which is to try you, as though some strange thing happened unto you."* Satan is never going to stop warring against the child of God.

2. We learn in this word that Satan's attacks are to weaken our faith or to destroy our faith. If we ever lose faith, we lose everything. In Luke, Chapter 22, Verses 31 and 32, Jesus said to Peter, *"Simon, Simon, behold, Satan has desired to have you, that he may sift you as wheat; But I have prayed for you, that your faith fail not."* Notice that the Lord didn't say, "I have prayed for you that *you* not fail," but He said He had prayed that Peter's *faith* not fail. It's one thing for us to fail, and we all do, but it's something else for our faith to fail.

3. Faith is the means by which God works in our lives— faith in Christ and what He did on Calvary's Cross.

Our faith is in Christ and the Cross and is the means by which all of His grace flows to us. Christ is the source, and the Cross is the means.

4. We find in this story that God allows Satan this latitude.
5. Trials are Satan's efforts to destroy us and God's efforts to build us up and to develop us.
6. We learn that trials are for our good, to bring us to a place of total dependence upon the Lord.

Again and again and again, Satan will come, but the Lord of Glory, the maker of heaven and earth, will not let Satan destroy us, but He will comfort us, help us, and restore to us if we don't give up.

Don't lose hope. You may be in the midst of an "again" situation, but remember, the Lord brought Job through, and He will bring you through.

CHURCH, READ
—THE—
BOOK OF ACTS
—AND—
GET READY!

CHAPTER 30

THE WORD *AGAIN* IN CHAPTER 2

The second chapter of Job begins with the word *again*: *"Again there was a day when the sons of God came to present themselves before the LORD, and Satan came also among them to present himself before the LORD"* (Job 2:1).

In this one word—*again*—there is a wealth of truth that we must all learn. This word tells us the following:

1. There is nothing the believer can do that will stop Satan from coming again and again to steal, kill, and destroy. I Peter 4:12 says, *"Beloved, think it not strange concerning the fiery trial which is to try you, as though some strange thing happened unto you."* Satan is never going to stop warring against the child of God.

2. We learn in this word that Satan's attacks are to weaken our faith or to destroy our faith. If we ever lose faith, we lose everything. In Luke, Chapter 22, Verses 31 and 32, Jesus said to Peter, *"Simon, Simon, behold, Satan has desired to have you, that he may sift you as wheat; But I have prayed for you, that your faith fail not."* Notice that the Lord didn't say, "I have prayed for you that *you* not fail," but He said He had prayed that Peter's *faith* not fail. It's one thing for us to fail, and we all do, but it's something else for our faith to fail.

3. Faith is the means by which God works in our lives— faith in Christ and what He did on Calvary's Cross.

Our faith is in Christ and the Cross and is the means by which all of His grace flows to us. Christ is the source, and the Cross is the means.

4. We find in this story that God allows Satan this latitude.

5. Trials are Satan's efforts to destroy us and God's efforts to build us up and to develop us.

6. We learn that trials are for our good, to bring us to a place of total dependence upon the Lord.

Again and again and again, Satan will come, but the Lord of Glory, the maker of heaven and earth, will not let Satan destroy us, but He will comfort us, help us, and restore to us if we don't give up.

Don't lose hope. You may be in the midst of an "again" situation, but remember, the Lord brought Job through, and He will bring you through.

WHO IS JESUS CHRIST?

"WHEN JESUS CAME INTO the coasts (borders) *of Caesarea Philippi* (about 30 miles north of the Sea of Galilee), *He asked His disciples, saying, Whom do men say that I the Son of Man am?* (The third form of unbelief manifested itself in popular indifference, indolence, or mere curiosity respecting the Messiah Himself. Upon the answer to this all-important question hinges the salvation of man.) *And they said, Some say that You are John the Baptist: some, Elijah; and others, Jeremiah, or one of the prophets* (this form of unbelief manifests itself in the frivolity of the natural heart). *He said unto them, But whom say you that I am?* (Addressed personally to the Twelve.) *And Simon Peter answered and said, You are the Christ, the Son of the living God* (the great confession)" (Mat. 16:13-16) (The Expositor's Study Bible).

On the night of Jan. 6, 1850, a young English lad was on his way to a scheduled appointment, only to find himself besieged by a snowstorm. As the snow and fierce winds beat against him, he looked for a place of shelter to get out of the storm.

Spying a dim light in the distance and thinking it to be an inn of some sort, he proceeded to enter, only to find himself in a Primitive Methodist chapel.

The weather was so bad that the pastor was not able to get to the service. As the handful of souls who had braved the bad weather sat in silence, a very thin man, a lowly shoemaker, stood up and went to the pulpit to fill in for the missing pastor.

It was obvious that this man was not an educated pastor, just a simple man. Opening his Bible, he read from Isaiah 45:22: *"Look unto Me, and be you saved, all the ends of the earth."*

The young man would later state that this common man could not even pronounce the words correctly, but that didn't really matter, for there was a power behind his simple words.

The message began with this dear humble man stating: "It says, 'look,' no looking don't take a deal of pain. It ain't lifting your foot or finger; it is just 'look.' Anyone can look, even a child can look. But then the text says, '*Look unto Me,*' look to Christ!"

The young man listening later said, "The eyes of this uneducated man looked right at me and said, 'Young man, look to Jesus Christ. Look! Look! Look! You have nothing to do but look.'"

The young man at once was convicted of his sin and accepted the Lord. That young man was none other than Charles Haddon Spurgeon, who would become one of England's greatest pastors.

THE QUESTION OF THE AGES

In the text we find the Lord asking His disciples the question, *"Whom do men say* (that) *I* (the Son of Man) *am?"* This one question constitutes the question of the ages. How one answers this question determines where one will spend eternity. How one answers this question determines what one really knows about Jesus Christ. How you answer that question determines who you are and where you are going.

THE CHURCH HAS FORGOTTEN WHO CHRIST IS

If one could somehow observe all the Sunday morning services in one's town, what kind of Jesus (if any) would be presented? In too many churches in America, the Jesus presented is not the Jesus of the Bible. In many churches, Christ is the great philosopher or He is the great environmentalist in the sky. In too many churches, Christ is just a good guy who wants to make you feel good about yourself and have a good laugh.

BUT WHOM SAY YOU THAT I AM?

Jesus was now speaking directly to His disciples. Now, understand that they had walked with Him, and they had seen His mighty works and miracles. Yet, He still asked the question. In effect, He was drawing them out, and today He is drawing you out.

Association and proximity to Christ doesn't mean one knows Christ. How many people sitting on our church pews really know who Christ is? There is only one correct answer.

YOU ARE THE CHRIST

Luke says in his account, *"The Christ of God"* (Lk. 9:20). Christ means "anointed" and in this sense, it referred to Him being the Messiah and King. Anointed means "to consecrate to a specific office," an office that only He could fulfill.

WHO IS JESUS CHRIST?

He is the Son of God and the Redeemer of mankind. He is the Anointed One, the specific One, and the unique One as King. He is the One Spurgeon called on and was saved. Who is Jesus Christ? One name or title doesn't do justice.

Who is Jesus Christ? The Word of God tells us:

- He is the seed of the woman, Jehovah, Shiloh, and the star out of Jacob.
- He is the prophet, King, Rock of salvation, the Anointed One, and the Son of God.
- He is the sanctuary, He is wonderful, He is Counselor, He is the mighty God, He is the Prince of Peace, and the everlasting Father.
- He is the root of Jesse, the branch, the polished shaft, and desire of all nations.

- He is sun of righteousness, refiner and purifier, the Son of Abraham, the Son of David, Master, Son of Man, the Great Physician, and our Sabbath rest.
- He is the bridegroom, the friend of sinners, horn of salvation, the Word, the Lamb of God, and the gift of God. He is the Bread of Life, He is the Light of the World, He is our Great Shepherd, He is the way, the truth, and He is the life.
- He is the door, He is the Passover, He is the author and finisher of our faith, He is a nail in a sure place, He is the morning star, He is the lion of the tribe of Judah, and He is the King of kings and Lord of lords.
- He is the Saviour, the healer, and the baptizer in the Holy Spirit. He is Christ, the Son of the living God, the only one who can redeem mankind from his sin and make that person a brand-new creation.

Who is Jesus Christ? He is my Saviour and my Lord, that's who Jesus Christ is.

CHURCH, READ
—— THE ——
BOOK OF ACTS
——AND——
GET READY!

CHAPTER 31

AMAZING GRACE

"*FOR BY GRACE* (the goodness of God) *are you saved through faith* (faith in Christ, with the Cross ever as its object)*; and that not of yourselves* (none of this is of us, but all is of Him)*: it is the gift of God* (anytime the word *gift* is used, God is speaking of His Son and His substitutionary work on the Cross, which makes all of this possible)*: Not of works* (man cannot merit salvation, irrespective of what he does)*, lest any man should boast* (boast in his own ability and strength; we are allowed to boast only in the Cross [Gal. 6:14])" (Eph. 2:8-9) (The Expositor's Study Bible).

EPHESUS

Ephesus was a celebrated city of Ionia in Asia Minor in what is now modern Turkey. The city was most known as the home of the temple of Diana, one of the seven wonders of the ancient world.

It was in this city of culture and pagan worship that Paul introduced the gospel of Jesus Christ in about the year

A.D. 54 (Acts 18:19). Though Paul would stay only a short time during his first visit, he would return for a period of about three years. It was during this time that the Ephesian church was established.

Paul remained at Ephesus preaching the gospel longer than he did at any other place. He probably stayed at Ephesus longer than his norm because this city was the principal seat of idolatry in the world. Paul, in writing Romans, Chapter 5, Verse 20, proclaimed, *"But where sin abounded, grace did much more abound."* How fitting it is that Paul would spend three years in this seat of idolatry proclaiming the good news of salvation through Jesus Christ.

GRACE

Paul proclaims in the text, *"For by grace are you saved."* It's interesting to note that in six chapters, Paul would use the word *grace* 12 times. I think it's obvious that the apostle proclaimed the doctrine of grace, which is the meaning of the new covenant, in a way that should be an example to all in ministry.

WHAT IS GRACE?

The theological definition of grace is "unmerited favor." It has been called "pure unrecompensed kindness and favor." However, a better explanation of the word *grace*, I feel, is "the goodness of God extended to undeserving believers." We deserved the wrath of God as all of us are born in sin, sons and daughters of Adam, but God in love and kindness has chosen to deal with sinful man on the basis of grace.

THE CROSS AND GRACE

There is no grace without the Cross. Grace always refers to the sacrificial offering of God's Son, Jesus Christ, on Calvary's Cross as the only remedy for man's sinful dilemma. Simply put, no Cross, no grace. That's why we can never cease proclaiming the Cross of Christ, and that's why we can never cease singing about the precious blood of God's Son, the Lamb slain before the foundation of the world.

The Cross is the supreme expression of grace. The gospel is its message, and only message, and we who are saved are trophies and witnesses of grace.

Grace is love in administration. Grace is love counteracting sin and seeking lost humanity's salvation.

Even more than an act, grace is a person—Jesus Christ. He alone is the embodiment of grace, the picture of grace, and the truth of grace, and the church must never forget that. Let us proclaim it to the world: Jesus Christ is grace, grace, amazing grace.

FAITH

The apostle states that grace is realized by the believing sinner through faith. Faith is the only means by which undeserving man can receive anything form the Lord. Faith, in the scriptural sense, means "belief and trust." It is believing and accepting what God has said in His Word. It is acceptance with all of one's heart.

Faith means that we place our past, present, and future hopes, dreams, and our entire being in Christ.

PROPER FAITH

By the term "proper faith" I mean that it is faith in what Christ did at the Cross for undeserving humanity. It is faith in His shed blood for salvation, healing, joy, etc. All that we have as Christians is because of Calvary. The Cross is to be the foundation, and the only foundation, of our faith.

NOT OF YOURSELVES

Paul clearly states that salvation is a gift of God. Man plays no part in salvation except for his expression of faith. Man is spiritually and morally bankrupt. There is nothing that is good and worthy in us. We are poor, doomed sons and daughters of Adam who deserve the wrath of just punishment by a holy and righteous judge, but, instead, we have been granted a reprieve through Jesus Christ.

Paul would boldly declare this in Ephesians 2:4-5: *"But God, who is rich in mercy, for His great love wherewith He loved us, even when we were dead in sins, has quickened us together with Christ, (by grace you are saved)."*

IT IS THE GIFT OF GOD

The Greek actually says, "And this is not out from you as a source, of God it is a gift." That is, salvation is a gift of God, and what a gift it is.

No matter how wicked and sinful man may be, and no matter how guilty and undeserving we are, the God of glory has a free gift for all who accept.

NOT OF WORKS

This proclaims the fact that salvation cannot be secured by any works of man. Paul would write in Romans 11:6: *"And if by grace, then is it no more of works: otherwise grace is no more grace. But if it be of works, then is it no more grace: otherwise work is no more work."* All human works and efforts are excluded from the equation.

Man loves works, especially his "good" works. Man has been deluded in the belief that he can save himself. Even after one is saved, the biggest battle of the soul is thinking that one can sanctify oneself through works. That is what the theme of Romans, Chapter 7, is. Oh, the folly of man who knows he can't save himself, yet he thinks he can sanctify himself through works. It has been said that the definition of insanity is doing the same thing over and over, expecting a different result each time. Yet, the church is continually trying to perfect sanctification by its own works, which is insanity when we have the Word of God plainly telling us that it's not of works.

LEST ANY MAN SHOULD BOAST

This statement presents the fact that while grace glorifies God, works glorify man. Works always produce self-righteousness. Boasting is a concept directly linked with one's understanding of himself and of God.

One should continually boast in the Lord. We should boast of His goodness, His grace, and His longsuffering, but never boast of ourselves.

As John Newton wrote it more than 200 years ago, grace is amazing.

CHURCH, READ
—— THE ——
BOOK OF ACTS
—— AND ——
GET READY!

CHAPTER 32

PERFECT PEACE

"YOU WILL KEEP HIM in perfect peace, whose mind is stayed on You: because he trusts in You. (The keynote of this passage is 'peace.' It speaks of the coming glad day of the millennium when Christ, the Prince of Peace, reigns supremely on earth. As well, every believer can presently enjoy the tremendous fruit of this promise by keeping our minds centered on Christ and what Christ has done for us at the Cross. This shows total and complete 'trust.')" (Isa. 26:3) (The Expositor's Study Bible).

The theme of this passage is peace. Its literal meaning concerns Israel during the millennium when Christ will be reigning, and Israel will have complete and perfect peace—spiritually, physically, and emotionally.

TWO TYPES OF PEACE

There is *justifying* peace and *sanctifying* peace.

Justifying peace is the peace that God gives when the believing sinner comes to Christ. The enmity of sin between

Christ and the sinner is removed because of what Christ did at Calvary and the sinner's acceptance of this finished work. Once we come to the Lord, justifying peace remains with us forever as we know our sins are gone, and we have made peace with God.

Sanctifying peace is something else completely. Whereas justifying peace never varies, sanctifying peace does so constantly. Sometimes it's up and sometimes it's down as it regards where our faith is placed.

Every single believer enjoys justifying peace, but most Christians don't enjoy sanctifying peace. That's the reason we have emotional disturbances, stress, fear, nervous disorders, depression, and a host of other upheavals in our minds.

WHY?

Most don't have sanctifying peace because of misplaced faith and a faulty understanding of grace. Actually, Paul constantly links peace with grace. To have perpetual peace, we must have an uninterrupted flow of grace in our lives. This is done by placing our faith exclusively in Christ and the Cross. When we begin to place our faith in other things, we *"frustrate the grace of God"* (Gal. 2:21). When grace is frustrated, sanctifying peace then stops. To have joy, peace of mind, and fulfillment, then one's faith must never move from Christ and Him crucified. Our faith must be placed 100 percent in Christ and what Christ did at the Cross. That and only that must be the object of our faith.

THE RENEWED MIND

The phrase, *"whose mind is stayed on You,"* refers to the renewed mind. The mind is the gateway to the Spirit. That on which we feed fills our minds constantly with that which is either fruitful or unfruitful. Simply put, to renew the mind refers to the believer pulling his faith from other things and placing it entirely in Christ and the Cross.

Paul addressed this in Romans 12:1-2: *"I beseech you therefore, brethren, by the mercies of God, that ye present your bodies a living sacrifice, holy, acceptable unto God, which is your reasonable service. And be not conformed to this world: but be ye transformed by the renewing of your mind, that ye may prove what is that good, and acceptable, and perfect, will of God."*

BECAUSE HE TRUSTS IN YOU

Let me repeat it once again regarding the Cross: to fully trust in the Lord is for our faith to be placed exclusively in Christ and the Cross and let nothing move us from that foundation.

Actually, we should do this on a daily basis. This is what Christ was meaning in Luke 9:23: *"And He said to them all, If any man will come after Me, let him deny himself, and take up his cross daily, and follow Me."*

CHURCH, READ
—— THE ——
BOOK OF ACTS
—— AND ——
GET READY!

CHAPTER 33

A BORROWED SHIP, AN EMPTY NET, AND THE WORD OF GOD

"*AND IT CAME TO pass, that, as the people pressed upon Him to hear the Word of God, He stood by the lake of Gennesaret* (the Sea of Galilee), *and saw two ships standing by the lake* (two among the many): *but the fishermen were gone out of them, and were washing their nets* (Peter, Andrew, James, and John had fished all night and caught nothing). *And he entered into one of the ships, which was Simon's* (proclaims Him borrowing this vessel to serve as a platform or pulpit), *and prayed him that he would thrust out a little from the land. And He sat down* (the custom then), *and taught the people out of the ship.*

"*Now when He had left speaking* (had finished preaching and teaching), *He said unto Simon, Launch out into the deep, and let down your nets for a draught* (came as a surprise to these fishermen; they had fished all night and caught nothing, so they must have wondered as to what He was doing; in effect, He will pay for the use of the boat; God will owe man nothing). *And Simon answering said unto Him, Master, we have toiled all night, and have taken nothing: nevertheless at Your word I will let down the net* (the idea is that Peter would not have bothered himself to have let down the net on the word of anyone else other than Jesus). *And when they had this done, they enclosed a great multitude of fishes: and their net broke* (so many fish that it broke the net). *And they beckoned unto their partners* (Peter and Andrew beckoned to James and John), *who were in the other ship, that they should come and help them. And they came, and filled both the ships, so that they began to sink* (Christ had the same power over the fish of the sea as He had over the frogs, lice, and locusts of Egypt).

"*When Simon Peter saw it* (proclaims the effect of this lesson is not to give Simon high thoughts of himself, but low thoughts; such is ever the effect of a manifestation of divine power and grace upon the conscience of fallen man), *he fell down at Jesus' knees, saying, Depart from me; for I am a sinful man, O Lord* (proclaims this miracle revealing the hidden unbelief of Simon's heart, for without a doubt, when casting the nets, he said to himself: 'We shall catch nothing'). *For he was astonished, and all who were with him, at the draught of the fishes which they had taken: And so was also James, and John, the sons of Zebedee, which were partners with Simon. And Jesus said unto Simon, Fear not; from henceforth you shall catch men* (the first recorded instance of Jesus using the words, 'fear not,' with His disciples; His statement elevated them to being fishers of men and constituted their call to discipleship and as apostles)" (Lk. 5:1-10) (The Expositor's Study Bible).

Every single thing the Lord did in His earthly ministry had a far greater meaning than meets the eye. As well, we must never forget that the great miracles performed by the Lord are just as available to us today as they were then.

THE PEOPLE CAME TO HEAR THE WORD OF GOD

The phrase, *"And it came to pass, that, as the people pressed upon Him to hear the Word of God,"* tells us the following:

1. Too many belittle preaching and exalt ceremony, but make no mistake, Jesus Christ, the Son of God, was the greatest preacher who ever lived. That's why Satan hates preaching under the anointing. True Bible preaching pulls no punches, takes no prisoners, and doesn't try to be diplomatic or politically correct. True Bible preaching preaches hell hot and heaven pure. True Bible preaching steps on toes and makes people uncomfortable at times. True Bible preaching is not philosophy but *"thus saith the Lord."*

2. The Word of God is the only revealed truth in the world today. There is no truth in Islam, Mormonism, Catholicism, Buddhism, Hinduism, or any other "ism" one can come up with. Not only must the Word of God be preached, but it also must be read and learned by the individual.

A BORROWED SHIP

As the crowd pressed in, pushing the Master closer to the water's edge, He saw the two ships of Peter, Andrew, James, and John.

The text says He got into Simon's ship, proclaiming the Master borrowing the ship to secure it as a platform or pulpit in order to preach to the masses gathered at the seashore.

LAUNCH OUT INTO THE DEEP, AND LET DOWN YOUR NETS FOR A DRAUGHT

After the Lord finished His time of ministry, He then turned to Simon and told him to, *"Launch out into the deep, and let down your nets for a draught."*

Now understand that they had fished all night and caught nothing; their nets were empty.

This is the lesson you must get into your spirit: the Lord wants to borrow your ship. Even though your net is empty, and your ship is in dry dock, the Lord wants to borrow what you have. I speak of your finances; this is how the work of the Lord is carried out (Rom. 10:13-15). Don't let an empty net stop you from receiving your miracle.

Never forget that the Lord never asks anything of anyone but that He gives back even in kind so much more than what we asked.

Your net may be empty, but the Creator of the sea and fish knows exactly where the fish are.

This was the Word of God to Simon: *"Launch out into the deep, and let down your nets for a draught."* And He is saying the same thing to you.

Don't let an empty net stand in your way. Let the Lord borrow your ship and let Him lead you to where the fish are.

NEVERTHELESS AT YOUR WORD I WILL LET DOWN THE NET

Faith is never inactive, but faith is always active, moving forward, and launching out into the deep.

So, what was about to happen was far more than a mere payment for kindness, but it was meant to serve as a lesson of faith for all of the body of Christ.

In the natural, Peter thought this was an impossible task, but that which is impossible with man is possible with God.

Peter's response was an act of faith. He obeyed the Word of the Lord.

What will you do? The same Lord who borrowed Peter's ship is asking to borrow your boat to help reach the lost masses of this world.

THE RESULT OF FAITH

Verse 6 says, *"And when they had this done, they enclosed a great multitude of fishes: and their net broke."*

Let me be plain: The Lord wants to break your net. He wants to bless you beyond your wildest dreams.

A SECOND SHIP

So many fish were in their net that the net was breaking, and they summoned another ship, referring to James and John. When the second ship arrived, there were so many fish that the ships began to sink. Why don't you let Him bless you, and why don't you let Him break your net? Why don't you go and get another boat to hold God's blessings?

The work of God must have everyone doing his part. Every one of you reading this has a ship the Lord wants to borrow. He knows your net may be empty, but if you will obey, He will bless you beyond your wildest dreams.

As the song says:

Why don't you let down your net down into the water,
There's a blessing waiting you cannot contain
Why don't you let down your net and wade out in the water,
He's pouring out the latter rain.

REFERENCES

Chapter 1

Donnie Swaggart, "Church, Read The Book Of Acts And Get Ready!" *The Evangelist*, February 2007.

Donnie Swaggart, "Church, Read The Book Of Acts And Get Ready! Part II" *The Evangelist*, March 2007.

Chapter 2

Donnie Swaggart, "The Vision Of Zechariah," *The Evangelist*, September 2007.

Chapter 3

Donnie Swaggart, "The River Of The Sanctuary," *The Evangelist*, April 2005.

Chapter 4

Donnie Swaggart, "The Wind And The Fire," *The Evangelist*, October 2005.

Chapter 5

Donnie Swaggart, "The Spirit Of Fear, The Spirit Of Power, The Spirit Of Love, The Spirit Of A Sound Mind" *The Evangelist*, December 2005.

Chapter 6
Donnie Swaggart, "The Spirit Makes Intercession," *The Evangelist*, November 2006.

Chapter 7
Donnie Swaggart, "The Power Of The Lord Was Present," *The Evangelist*, December 2006.

Chapter 8
Donnie Swaggart, "The Holy Spirit Fell," *The Evangelist*, April 2007.

Chapter 9
Donnie Swaggart, "This Is That," *The Evangelist*, May 2007.

Chapter 10
Donnie Swaggart, "Have You Received The Holy Spirit Since You Believed?" *The Evangelist*, July 2007.

Chapter 11
Donnie Swaggart, "The Rest And The Refreshing," *The Evangelist*, February 2008.

Chapter 12
Donnie Swaggart, "Fill Thine Horn With Oil And Go," *The Evangelist*, December 2008.

Chapter 13
Donnie Swaggart, "Follow The Man Bearing A Pitcher Of Water," *The Evangelist*, March 2009.

Chapter 14
Donnie Swaggart, "The Power Of Pentecost," *The Evangelist*, August 2009.

Chapter 15
Donnie Swaggart, "The Benefits Of Speaking In Other Tongues," *The Evangelist*, October 2009.

Chapter 16
Donnie Swaggart, "The Spirit Of The Lord Is Upon Me," *The Evangelist*, August 2010.

Chapter 17
Donnie Swaggart, "He Has Anointed Me To Preach The Gospel," *The Evangelist*, September 2010.

Chapter 18
Donnie Swaggart, "There Is A River," *The Evangelist*, July 2009.

Chapter 19
Donnie Swaggart, "Saul Was Refreshed And Well," *The Evangelist*, October 2008.

Chapter 20
Donnie Swaggart, "These Men Do Exceedingly Trouble Our City," *The Evangelist*, June 2007.

Chapter 21
Donnie Swaggart, "The River," *The Evangelist*, November 2014.

Chapter 22
Donnie Swaggart, "What About The Wind And The Fire?" *The Evangelist*, January 2011.

Chapter 23
Donnie Swaggart, "The Function Of The Holy Spirit," *The Evangelist*, August 2011.

Chapter 24
Donnie Swaggart, "Seven Steps To Receiving The Holy Spirit," *The Evangelist*, March 2012.

Chapter 25
Donnie Swaggart, "I Will Pour Water Upon Him Who Is Thirsty," *The Evangelist*, November 2012.

Chapter 26
Donnie Swaggart, "The Day Of Pentecost," *The Evangelist*, June 2013.

Chapter 27
Donnie Swaggart, "The Altar, The Lamp, The Oil," *The Evangelist*, July 2014.

Chapter 28
Donnie Swaggart, "The Precious Blood Of Christ," *The Evangelist*, February 2011.

Chapter 29
Donnie Swaggart, "Again," *The Evangelist*, March 2011.

Chapter 30
Donnie Swaggart, "Who Is Jesus Christ?" *The Evangelist*, April 2011.

Chapter 31
Donnie Swaggart, "Amazing Grace," *The Evangelist*, May 2011.

Chapter 32
Donnie Swaggart, "Perfect Peace," *The Evangelist*, June 2011.

Chapter 33
Donnie Swaggart, "A Borrowed Ship, An Empty Net, And The Word Of God," *The Evangelist*, July 2011.

ABOUT EVANGELIST DONNIE SWAGGART

 Evangelist Donnie Swaggart has been preaching the gospel to audiences around the world for more than 30 years. Having grown up literally on the evangelistic circuit, Brother Donnie traveled the globe with his parents, Evangelist Jimmy and Frances Swaggart, as their ministry audience grew from small rural churches in the United States to crusades that filled some of the world's largest coliseums.

In the 1980s, Brother Donnie was the primary architect of the Jimmy Swaggart crusades. His responsibilities included contracting meeting venues, national and international transport of all equipment necessary for the crusade team and sound stage, and oversight of the sales and distribution of ministry products.

When Family Worship Center, the home church of Jimmy Swaggart Ministries, opened in 1984, Brother Donnie was named co-pastor of the 4,000-seat facility where he ministers regularly including three annual campmeetings.

Known for his fiery preaching style and fervor for Pentecost, Brother Donnie maintains a robust evangelistic schedule, preaching four rallies each year in the United States as well as outreaches to Africa, Australia, Canada, Europe, and South America.

In 2010, Jimmy Swaggart Ministries launched the SonLife Broadcasting Network (SBN), which airs 24 hours a day and is now available to a potential audience of 280 million homes worldwide.

Instrumental in the establishment and ongoing administrations of the network, Brother Donnie also serves as a regular panelist on *Frances & Friends*—SBN's interactive talk show that addresses issues of interest to the church. He also hosts the network's newest program, *Preachers, Patriots & Providence*.

Brother Donnie and his wife, Debbie, live in Baton Rouge, Louisiana. They have three grown children—Jennifer, Gabriel, and Matthew—and eight grandchildren. This is his first book.